THE
New
ELEMENTARY
Teacher's
HANDBOOK
Third Edition

This book is dedicated to my daughters, Lauren, Lisa, and Dana, who, through the joy of parenting, taught me the true meaning of listening, sharing, learning, and teaching.

Nancy

To Joe for his unwavering support and love; to Paige and Madison for all they teach me about life and living; and to my sister Cindi for potluck Fridays.

Mary

THE
New
ELEMENTARY
Teacher's
HANDBOOK
Third Edition

Flourishing in Your First Year

Kathleen Jonson

Nancy Cappelloni

Mary Niesyn

CORWIN
A SAGE Company

For information:

Corwin
A SAGE Company
2455 Teller Road
Thousand Oaks, California 91320
(800) 233–9936
Fax: (800) 417–2466
www.corwin.com

SAGE Ltd.
1 Oliver's Yard
55 City Road
London EC1Y 1SP
United Kingdom

SAGE India Pvt. Ltd.
B 1/I 1 Mohan Cooperative
    Industrial Area
Mathura Road, New Delhi 110 044
India

SAGE Asia-Pacific Pte. Ltd.
33 Pekin Street #02-01
Far East Square
Singapore 048763

Printed in the United States of America

Library of Congress Cataloging-in-Publication Data

Jonson, Kathleen Feeney.
The new elementary teacher's handbook : flourishing in your first year / Kathleen Jonson, Nancy Cappelloni, and Mary Niesyn. — 3rd ed.
        p. cm.
Includes bibliographical references and index.
ISBN 978-1-4129-7809-5 (pbk.)

    1. First year teachers—United States—Handbooks, manuals, etc. 2. Elementary school teachers—United States—Handbooks, manuals, etc. 3. Elementary school teaching—United States—Handbooks, manuals, etc. I. Cappelloni, Nancy. II. Niesyn, Mary. III. Title.

LB2844.1.N4J65 2011
372.11—dc22   2010031505

This book is printed on acid-free paper.

10   11   12   13   14   10   9   8   7   6   5   4   3   2   1

Acquisitions Editor:	Dan Alpert
Associate Editor:	Megan Bedell
Editorial Assistant:	Sarah Bartlett
Production Editor:	Amy Schroller
Copy Editor:	Adam Dunham
Permissions Editor:	Karen Ehrmann
Typesetter:	C&M Digitals (P) Ltd.
Proofreader:	Victoria Reed-Castro
Cover Designer:	Rose Storey

Contents

Preface to the Third Edition

2010 marks a challenging time in the education of children in this nation. The last decade was one that will be recognized by an increase in accountability, practices and policies related to No Child Left Behind (2008), the exciting new uses of technology in the classroom intended to inspire and challenge a new generation of learners, a greater diversity in the ethnic and cultural makeup of our schools, and a new focus on *professional learning communities.*

The economic strain we are currently experiencing has taken a toll on the youngest members of our population. Increased cutbacks in school funding have affected all aspects of education for our youngest to oldest students. Reduced class size is becoming a remnant of the past. Teachers are faced with greater academic expectations and an increase in desired student outcomes, continued scrutiny of teacher effectiveness, and greater accountability, while they are being given more students in the classrooms with the expectation to differentiate instruction for all learners.

The third edition of *The New Elementary Teacher's Handbook* contains new material taking into account this changing context of education. The *Handbook* realistically discusses the challenges elementary classroom teachers face today. New resources have been added to the end of each chapter to provide practical, ready-to-use ideas for new teachers. Current references, websites, and book lists add to the relevancy of teaching in today's classrooms.

New teachers are diamonds in the rough. As new teachers, you bring new energy, enthusiasm, hope, optimism, ideas, idealism, and commitment to the profession. As your experience builds, your teaching becomes enhanced through your experiences and new knowledge. We, as veteran teachers and mentors, need to keep your spirit alive, support you in the best way we can, and realize the enormous value and contribution you make in the education of our most precious commodity—the children in this nation.

Acknowledgments

We would like to express our deep gratitude and appreciation to those who have given us the support and encouragement needed during the process of completing this book.

We are especially grateful for the patience and understanding of our families, who believe in what we do and understand the aspirations we have for ourselves. We are grateful for the many colleagues we have who, through their collective wisdom, guidance, and expertise, have helped and supported us professionally through the years. We would also like to extend our sincerest appreciation to our editor, Dan Alpert, for his continued encouragement and enthusiasm for this book without whom this book would not have been possible.

Publisher's Acknowledgments

Corwin gratefully acknowledges the contributions of the following reviewers:

Juan Araujo, Lecturer
College of Education
University of North Texas
Denton, TX

Patricia Baker, K–5 Teacher
Fauquier County Public Schools
Culpeper, VA

Anita Barnes, Elementary School Teacher
Frankfort, KY

Nancy Betler, Instructional Support Specialist, PreK–12 Literacy
Charlotte Mecklenburg Schools
Charlotte, NC

Emmalee Callaway, Second-Grade Discovery Teacher
Acres Green Elementary School
Parker, CO

Lorie Cook-Benjamin, Professor of Teacher Education
Fort Hays State University
Hays, KS

About the Authors

In her 40 years as an educator, **Dr. Kathleen Jonson**, professor emerita, taught at the elementary and secondary levels, and served as a reading specialist, director of staff development, principal, director of curriculum and instruction, and university faculty. She conducted numerous workshops for teachers and administrators on such topics as reading comprehension strategies, writing process, portfolio assessment, peer coaching, and beginning teacher assistance programs. Until her retirement in summer 2009, Dr. Jonson was professor of education and coordinator of the Master in Arts in Teaching Reading program in the School of Education of the University of San Francisco, in San Francisco, California. She published three books with Corwin, including *The New Elementary Teacher's Handbook* (1st edition, 1997; 2nd edition, 2001), *Being an Effective Mentor: How to Help Beginning Teachers Succeed* (1st edition, 2002; 2nd edition, 2007), and *60 Strategies for Improving Reading Comprehension in Grades K–8* (2006).

Dr. Jonson and her husband divide their time between California and a small island north of Seattle, Washington.

Nancy Cappelloni, EdD, has taught at the elementary level and in early childhood education for the past 20 years. Currently, she is an adjunct professor in the teacher education department at the University of San Francisco, teaches kindergarten, and conducts numerous professional development workshops for teachers and parents on topics such as early literacy, self-regulated learning, and kindergarten readiness. Dr. Cappelloni is an educational consultant, working with young children with learning challenges, and she works collaboratively with the child's family and school to create an integrative intervention system and partnership. Dr. Cappelloni is the author of a children's cookbook, *Ethnic Cooking the Microwave Way,* and a book on cranberries, *Cranberry Cooking for All Seasons.* Her management experience as the director of Tiburon/Belvedere's Park and Recreation Department and as a dance/movement therapist working with children with special needs brings her a unique perspective of diverse educational environments, community programs, and children with special needs. Dr. Cappelloni is a member of a number of professional affiliations and memberships, including Phi Delta Kappa International and the American

Educational Research Association. Her research interests include self-regulated learning strategies, kindergarten readiness, early learning standards in early childhood education, and emergent literacy.

 **Mary Niesyn, MS,** is an elementary teacher, a teacher consultant for the Bay Area Writing Project at the University of California, Berkeley, and a part-time faculty member in the School of Education for both the University of San Francisco and Dominican University. In her role as elementary teacher, she has been a mentor teacher, a master teacher, and a beginning teacher support and assessment (BTSA) provider. She is also a trained assessor in California's Teacher Performance Assessments (TPAs). For over a decade, she has facilitated numerous workshops and professional development seminars focused on best practices in early literacy. As a writing consultant, she has provided professional development on writing instruction to educators both nationally and internationally. In addition to coauthoring this handbook for teachers, she is the author of a professional development in-service guide (2009) and publications for academic journals. Her research interests include best practices in literacy instruction, teacher education, and professional development.

1

You Are Not Alone

Welcome to the teaching profession! Often named the noblest of all professions, teaching is certainly among the most important jobs in the world. No one can doubt that teachers have broad, long-lasting impact on the lives of children. A deeper purpose, a larger vision of service motivates most new teachers—not money or prestige (though both should be greater!). The work is indeed rewarding. Nothing quite compares to a student's face lighting up to learning, or having a student you taught years ago come back to visit you in your classroom. Teaching is about facilitating learning, growing, and developing. Teaching provides you the opportunity to make a difference in the lives of children as they acquire the skills and knowledge to learn effectively and successfully in school.

As you interact with students during your hectic beginning years, stay in touch with the reasons that brought you to teaching in the first place. You, too, are beginning on a new path of learning and growth. Much of the time, you will be working alone in your classroom with little opportunity to pause and reflect on your new role as a teacher. You may at times feel isolated, insecure, and unsure of your abilities. Stop to reflect on your strengths, acknowledge what you do well, and focus on what needs to be accomplished. Try not to become too overwhelmed by all that there is to do, because teaching is like housework—there is always more you can do! Establish priorities, and focus on important tasks first. One new teacher was told by her mentor to first get through each day, and then begin to plan for a week. Before you know it, you can plan an entire unit, month, or even trimester! Few people will ever understand how hard you work, how much physical and emotional energy you put into your job, or the multifaceted role you serve as an elementary school teacher. Although you may occasionally receive a compliment or an encouraging word, few adults will know the fine job you do inside the classroom and the attention you pay to each student. Even your caring, compassion, and concern for children, the core reasons you became a teacher, may go unnoticed. But, stay positive, even when the going gets tough. Don't be discouraged. There will be many ups and downs. You will doubt your judgment and decisions frequently. It is important to guard against becoming disheartened during the frenzied pace of the first year. But, give yourself credit for all the wonderful things you are doing for your students, too. Relax, and have some fun. Laugh a little! Enjoy the students and all the wonderful things they have to offer you. Continue your good work. You are on your way to actualizing an important mission—a claim few other professions can make.

After the scrutiny of a lengthy student-teaching and credentialing process, you may, as many new teachers report, feel suddenly adrift. You are on your own. No university faculty or supervisors are there to provide a safety net. No friendly, familiar faces can be counted on for advice. In the months ahead, you need to find new sources of support from people who can help and support you to prosper as a teacher. These mentors and colleagues will show you how to navigate the complexities of the school system. They will welcome you personally and professionally and will provide a social and emotional support system. You are not alone. As you become better acquainted with the teachers, staff, and community of your new school, you will gradually learn what you need to know. You will refine your vision of what it means to be a teacher, and your personal philosophy of teaching will emerge. You will move toward a greater sense of teacher efficacy and confidence when you say to yourself, "I know I can teach any and all of these kids!" You will grow professionally and personally, becoming more comfortable with your new teaching role and professional responsibilities. Indulge yourself during this process to experience all that you can, try new things, challenge yourself, and take risks, knowing that you will become a stronger, better teacher for the children entrusted to your care.

BASIC EMPLOYEE INFORMATION

Make sure you have the following basic employee information:

- Copy of your contract
- School and district rosters
- Benefit forms
- District calendar
- Current curriculum vitae (CV)

Start a special file folder for your key professional documents. Keep it handy, and update it each year. Begin a second file for copies of your formal and informal evaluations, your annual goals, any professional development training, and copies of transcripts from recent coursework. Keep dated receipts for purchases made for your classroom. You may not get reimbursed, but save them for your taxes.

FITTING IN

Visit your assigned school at least one or two weeks before classes begin. It is important to learn about the social and cultural climate of your school and the surrounding neighborhood. Get to know the community. Subscribe to a local newspaper. Familiarize yourself with the attendance boundaries of this particular school, and then walk through the neighborhoods and shops. Think about the backgrounds, socioeconomic status, cultures, ethnicities, languages, and demographics represented in the community. Perhaps your school draws from several neighborhoods. How do these neighborhoods contrast?

Now, take a walk around the school, both inside and out. You probably have toured the school during your job interview, but perhaps you did not get to spend much time feeling your way around. You will sense your school's climate the minute you enter it. Is the atmosphere conducive to learning? Does it feel like a caring, student-friendly place? Does it feel student centered or teacher centered? Tour the halls, and look into classrooms. Locate the library, resource center, the computer lab or technology center, the teachers' workroom, the multipurpose room/stage, art room, the teachers' and students' restrooms, and the main office. You will see many new faces. Don't be shy. Stop in to say hello to the principal. In most schools, you will be assigned a mentor. Confer with the principal about who this will be, and get to know the mentor. Your mentor will be an excellent resource, especially at the beginning of the year when you have *a lot* of questions. Get to know the administrative assistants and the custodians. They will be important people in your life! Introduce yourself to all classified and certificated staff members you happen to meet. Visiting your new school as often as possible before the opening day provides you with an excellent opportunity to meet your new colleagues before they are faced with their own day-to-day teaching demands. Use the School Roster (Resource 1.1) form to make notes. Allow yourself some unstructured time to get a feel for the school before you're engulfed in opening-week staff meetings, orientation sessions, and setting up your own classroom and preparing for the first days of school.

As you meet colleagues, you will begin to learn not only names and roles but also the informal norms and expectations of your new workplace. In some schools, beginning teachers find an open, welcoming atmosphere. In others, staff members act toward one another in a more private, reserved manner. The social context of the school—its subtle web of unwritten rules, values, expectations, and relationships among staff members, students, and parents, and their personal backgrounds—will directly influence your teaching and your interactions with colleagues and students. But, be yourself, and try to feel comfortable in your new surroundings. Take time to observe, and refrain from making snap judgments. As you listen and learn, continue to get along with everyone.

In addition to physically spending time at your new school, be sure to visit the district and school virtually. Most districts and individual school sites have websites full of rich information, including school and district policies, mission statements, special programs, school calendars, and employee profiles. You may even find photos of schoolwide events and celebrations. In many schools, individual teachers have classroom websites.

Exploring these sites is an excellent way to familiarize yourself with the culture and learning expectations of your new school.

Strategies to Help You Fit In

- Learn names immediately—study the staff roster, and practice pronouncing each name aloud. Create and post a photo poster in your classroom of familiar faces and names. Include aides, custodians, yard duty personnel, librarians, and other support staff. This handy reference will be invaluable to both you and your students.
- Use good manners.
- Dress professionally. Your attire is very important—it shows respect for yourself, your school, and the profession. Some schools reserve Fridays for casual dress wear or school spirit wear. Find out your school's protocol for these special days, and be sure to participate.
- Become acquainted with one or more teachers in neighboring classrooms and with those who teach the same grade level you do. Enjoy their company, and find something similar in your backgrounds. Ask about regular grade-level meetings, and find out who your grade-level coordinator is.
- Compliment a teacher who has an especially attractive, well-arranged classroom. Ask for tips, and be generous with compliments. Offer to share something that another teacher might like in your room.
- Make it a point to hand in requested paperwork and online forms to the office on time. Make sure you know your duty-assignment schedule and policies (recess or playground, bus, and lunchtime duty).
- Visit the faculty room, and regularly eat lunch with the other teachers—don't get in the habit of eating lunch isolated in your classroom to catch up on paperwork. This provides an important time to get to know other teachers, to listen and share ideas (be careful not to talk about other teachers), and to bond.
- Be open to sharing ideas and resources.
- When you are assigned to recess duty, be on time and be alert. Take the opportunity to watch students interact. As a new teacher, your familiarity with students other than those in your class will be limited. Get to know students from a variety of grade levels. Don't talk to other adults unnecessarily while you are on duty. Your responsibility is first and foremost the safety of the students.
- Make sure your students do not roam the halls distracting others—avoid excusing them from your classroom unnecessarily with bathroom passes, library passes, or various errands.
- Join your local teachers' association, even if your district doesn't require it. Begin learning about association bargaining and politics, but don't get involved your first year.
- Join your "Rainbow Club" or social club. Contribute money cheerfully for faculty birthday gifts, cards, flowers, wedding, new faculty, and baby or hospital remembrances.
- Avoid cliques. Don't repeat rumors, complain, or spread gossip.
- Avoid taking sides on issues until you have had a chance to think them through carefully.

- Establish excellent rapport with your school administrators early in the school year. If you say you will do something, do it.
- Don't join extra committees if you are not required to do so the first year, but helping out here and there with extra assignments will really give you bonus points!
- Find out who's who in the district administration. You may not see these people often, but you should know their names and roles. See Resource 1.2, School District Roster.
- Observe how staff members interact with each other, with the principal, with students, and with parents.
- Strive to do a good job—give it your all. Your efforts will be noticed, and you will become known as a conscientious worker and a positive addition to your school community.
- Learn how much input parents have into the programs of the school.
- Take note of the teachers' attitudes toward students, parents, and the community.
- Find out to what extent teachers criticize policies and practices of the school or central office administration.

As you apply yourself to these strategies, you will get a better understanding of your school's inner workings. You will also discover which teachers your principal often calls on for assistance, listens to, and what is expected from them in return. Do you feel an easy camaraderie with these teachers? If so, consider yourself fortunate. At the same time, be careful. You do not know these teachers well yet. If they object to something you may be doing at school, these teachers can easily report their observations to the principal without your knowledge. Make sure you allow enough time to find out who is who on your school's staff before you confide in, complain to, or criticize anyone.

Norms and Expectations

Learning what is expected, both formally and informally, is a crucial part of fitting into your new workplace. Learn your school's norms and expectations. Some of these are described in your contract, handbooks, and school policies.

- Learn the procedures for student discipline, parent communication, and student reporting, maintaining student records, phone and e-mail communication procedures, and confidentiality.
- Learn the expectations and policies regarding playground and lunch duty, tardy and absentee procedures, staff meetings, parent conferences, religious observances, teacher work days, visitor sign in and strangers on campus, sick leave and substitutes, and fire, earthquake, hurricane, or other disaster and emergency procedures.

Many recent reform movements are trying to encourage teachers to work together more closely. One such reform currently taking hold in many districts across the nation is the formation of *professional learning communities* (PLCs).

Professional Learning Communities

The 1980s marked the beginning of the research and implementation of *professional learning communities*. The idea grew out of research suggesting that teachers who felt supported by means of teacher networks, cooperation among colleagues, and expanded professional roles increased their own sense of teacher efficacy and were more likely to remain in the profession. The implementation of a PLC model can and will look different among districts and even individual school sites. The overall goal, however, is the same—to assist teachers to work collaboratively on planning instruction, observing in each other's classrooms, and sharing feedback. This is great news for teachers such as yourself, and it is an exciting time to be entering the profession.

Five Attributes of Professional Learning Communities

- Supportive and shared leadership
- Collective creativity
- Shared values and vision
- Supportive conditions
- Shared personal practice

ESTABLISHING RELATIONSHIPS TO HELP YOU SUCCEED

New teachers may seek help from many sources, depending on the need. Begin with your mentor if you have one, your grade-level coordinator, or other grade-level teachers. Your principal will assist you with challenging situations regarding students and parents. Feel free to turn to the teacher in a neighboring classroom or to any other friendly colleague. In most cases, you can get needed information or suggestions by asking someone directly. Most teachers will be genuinely interested in helping whenever possible. Determine the best time of day to approach staff members or others. In emergencies, of course, seek help immediately! In other cases, you may choose to wait until lunch or break times, the end of the school day, or maybe even the following morning. Give teachers time to respond to your questions or requests. When you are sensitive to others' schedules, you will find they have more time and appear more relaxed and ready to answer questions. If you feel uncomfortable, preface your inquiry with an opener such as

"I've been wondering . . ."

"Would you know . . ."

"I still don't understand . . ."

"I haven't seen anything about . . ."

"Have you received . . ."

"I've noticed that . . ."

The following sections provide information on how to establish good working relationships with the principal, staff members, and others who can help you succeed.

The Principal

The principal has a strong influence on the climate of the school. Most principals are effective, competent instructional leaders who will be able to help you with student-management issues, parent issues, and with a myriad of other concerns. Your principal is responsible for everything and everyone in the school. Think of your principal as your ally. You can expect your principal to be fair and supportive of teachers and to have students' best interests in mind. Your principal is there to give you as much support during your first year as possible, but because of the vast responsibilities of that position, your principal may not be as available to you as you might wish.

Find out if you are required to make an appointment to see the principal or if you can approach the principal in the hallway, send notes or e-mails, or meet before or after school. Ask your principal what types of behavioral and discipline situations or issues with parents she needs to know about. If you're not sure, ask. Become familiar with your school's policies regarding injuries and other emergencies. You are typically required to inform the principal immediately about injuries, emergencies, or other urgent situations.

Usually, the principal or assistant principal evaluates teachers. Find out what the procedures are for your evaluation. Find out which administrator is responsible, what the evaluation form looks like, what you are expected to do (such as perform a particular lesson in your class), and when and how frequently you will be evaluated. In addition to formal evaluations, your principal may informally visit your classroom without prior notice, especially during your first year. Become accustomed to such visits. A quick acknowledgment of the principal's arrival will let the students know you welcome the visit. Then, continue with business as usual. The principal will quietly move about the room, perhaps interacting with a student or two. After a few visits, you will become quite comfortable and feel much more at ease being observed. This increased sense of confidence will carry over during formal observations.

During your orientation meeting, the principal will usually review many of the items on the School Information Checklist (see Resource 1.3) as well as other questions and concerns you and other new teachers may have. Ask questions—do not rely on assumptions. Using the information obtained at this meeting, develop your own To Do list, consisting of forms to complete, deadlines, after-hours building use, parking, lesson plan and scheduling requirements, and many other things you will need to do and know. Post the checklist and supporting information near your desk, and work your way through it from the most urgent items to the least.

Mentors

Experienced teachers are logical sources of assistance, support, and feedback for beginning teachers. Many school systems are now providing all their new teachers with mentors. Mentoring is an effective way to support and retain capable new teachers, as well as to assist them in improving their teaching abilities. One of the most important staff relationships you will develop will be with your mentor. Typically, mentors are teachers with several years of experience at your school and grade level. Even if your mentor happens to now teach a lower or higher grade, your mentor will still be familiar with your students' age level and perhaps with many of your students' families. Feel fortunate if you are employed in a school in which you can count on help from an experienced colleague assigned to provide professional advice and assistance. Such a mentor provides tremendous teaching as well as emotional support for you as you deal with the concerns, challenges, and issues of a beginner teacher. Ask your principal if your school offers new teachers mentors formally. If not, find an experienced colleague you have become friendly with. Mention that you could use some suggestions on grouping certain students, for instance, or ideas about how to handle a recent classroom management problem. Assure this colleague that you will not need a great deal of time. Be clear about what you are asking for—that you could learn a lot about teaching reading from the colleague, for example, or that you would love to hear more about her students' successful work with math manipulatives. Find common ground. Be genuine and gracious. Remark that you are hoping for a chance to work more closely with someone, and that you will truly appreciate any time she is able to spare.

If your colleague agrees, you may have found an invaluable support. When someone expresses interest in helping, you may have found a mentor. On the other hand, he may politely decline, citing other commitments that make it difficult to consult with you. In that case, go ahead and approach other colleagues. Your respectful inquiries will be rewarded eventually.

New-Teacher Induction Programs

While many schools cannot provide individual mentors for each new teacher, many schools and districts will have a formal induction program in place. Induction programs are typically two-year training and support programs for new teachers. Such programs are mandated in many states. Your support provider may or may not work at your site. Some support providers no longer work in classrooms. However, be assured that all support providers have been formally trained in the induction program and are eager to work with you. Be sure to ask your principal if you are eligible for participation in a new-teacher induction program.

A Good Mentor-Protégé Relationship

Working with a mentor is like having a friend who understands anxieties and concerns about teaching. Your mentor is also familiar with all those subtle nuances of your school and its informal and formal norms. In return, you must establish a good relationship with your mentor. Much will depend on the respect the two of you develop for each other.

Research on mentor-protégé relationships has found that their success is generally based on two major factors: (1) whether the protégé respects the mentor as a person, and (2) whether the protégé admires the mentor's knowledge, experience, and style. By the same token, a mentor must feel comfortable working with a new teacher. Ideally, a new teacher and mentor will get along both personally and professionally.

The following traits characterize the sort of person who becomes a good new-teacher protégé. Check off all those traits you already possess.

_____ Has a positive, proactive attitude

_____ Is complimentary more often than critical in interactions with others

_____ Can take constructive criticism positively

_____ Can self-reflect and even laugh at self

_____ Is conscientious and well organized

_____ Is ambitious and shows determination and perseverance

_____ Has a willingness to accept new challenges

_____ Accepts responsibility for self, class, and students

Other Classroom Teachers

As a new teacher, you will find that your colleagues' attitudes and interactions help set the climate of the school. Some schools will, as a whole, be more welcoming and nurturing to newcomers than others. Most often, you will find a supportive faculty willing to share materials and ideas and serve as informal mentors. Look for collegiality with teachers who are positive and helpful while avoiding those who seem negative. As you demonstrate your competence and willingness to learn, you will gradually gain acceptance. Remember, you are launching your professional career, not just your first class.

Similar to schoolwide projects, many schools require all teachers to volunteer for schoolwide committee work. These committees are part of the day-to-day functioning of the school. Some principals exempt first-year teachers from such requirements. Find out the protocol at your school, and be ready to volunteer if it is required. You may look to your principal or mentor teacher for advice in selecting the right committee—one that does not require prior experience or an enormous amount of time.

Do offer to help with schoolwide projects—it is important to spend some time and energy making a positive impact on your school as a whole. Pick one significant project that interests you and that will allow you to network with professional colleagues. Your contribution will be noticed. But, also learn to say no, refusing to allow too many extras to be added to your assignment. You might also be tutoring students after school, or you may be taking graduate courses one or two nights a week. You also need time to take care of yourself. Avoid overextending yourself in your first years.

Classified Staff Members

All classified staff members in the building have roles that directly or indirectly affect students' learning and the climate of the school. It is important to treat classified staff members with the utmost courtesy and respect. They often know much about their school and community and can be wonderful resources for a new teacher.

Administrative Assistants

These invaluable staff members have a great deal of informal authority and often have the last word on how things need to be done, school procedures, and many of the "where, when, whats, and hows" that you will need to know on a daily basis! These include details such as field-trip and driver forms, reimbursements, supplies, substitute procedures, setting the school alarm, use of office equipment (such as the photocopy machine), attendance procedures, reduced-price lunches, location of cumulative records ("cum files"), and various parent and teacher forms.

Custodians

Do not overlook the importance of these staff members! Establish a positive relationship with custodians by letting them know you are most appreciative of the work they do, and try to cooperate with their procedures. Find out how they want to have things done.

- How do custodians want the classroom to look at the end of the school day? Should chairs be placed on the desks? Should whiteboards be cleaned? Should tables be cleared?
- What are the procedures for dealing with spills or young children's "accidents"?
- What is the procedure for making needed classroom repairs? Will custodians be available to make minor repairs, or is a separate maintenance request required for these tasks?
- What is the procedure for getting new supplies, furniture, and equipment in the room?
- How do you obtain such items as classroom paper towels, soap, hand sanitizer, and sponges?

Instructional Aides

Instructional aides, or educational support personnel, are important assistants working under your direction. Although in many schools instructional aides are not assigned to each classroom, many teachers will reap the benefits of the additional instructional support they can provide for an hour or more per day. Instructional aides can help with certain types of instruction, such as working with individual children or with small groups of students. Some schools require aides to spend all their time working directly with students. In other schools, aides divide their time between noninstructional activities and working directly with students. Be sure to find out the expectations in your school.

Instructional activities you might assign to aides could include the following:

- Providing small groups of students with support in specific subjects
- Helping students who were absent catch up on missed work
- Helping students with class projects
- Helping struggling students with assignments
- Checking work and responding in writing to student journals
- Working with a small group directing an activity

Noninstructional activities might include the following:

- Helping with record keeping, portfolios, and filing
- Preparing bulletin boards and other instructional materials
- Duplicating, gathering, and distributing materials

If you have the assistance of an instructional aide, it may be that the time spent together is limited, and there is not time to meet without students. If at all possible, however,

- Allow time for you and your aide to meet and exchange introductions, to share your educational philosophy and teaching priorities, and to establish good rapport;
- As you train your aide for tasks, model as well as explain;
- Remember also that teacher aides observe what goes on in the classroom and interact with parents and other school staff; insist that your aide respect the confidentiality of students and interactions in the classroom at all times;
- Create a positive and cooperative classroom atmosphere; your students need to see you and your aide working together as a team— give your aide stature as your "assistant teacher"; and
- Always provide specific, helpful feedback that acknowledges good efforts and successful approaches, even when suggesting strategies for improvement.

Volunteers

Volunteers may include parents, high school and college students, and community members. Parents may comprise the most frequent volunteers in the classroom, depending on your school. In some communities, volunteers are more available than in others, depending on family structures, parent commitments, and the parents' employment status. Volunteers can provide valuable extra assistance and attention to students who may need additional support. Many teachers invite volunteers to share special talents, such as teaching art or discussing careers. Some teachers use volunteers only for short times or special projects or for assistance with noninstructional classroom responsibilities. Your school is likely to have policies or informal norms regarding the use of volunteers. Find out what these expectations are from your administrator and mentor. Then, consider the following strategies for working successfully with volunteers:

1. Discuss whether you and your students would be likely to benefit from volunteers in your classroom. For instance, would volunteers be especially helpful for certain subjects or times of the day?

2. Find out if your school district has a well-established volunteer program and, if so, how it works and how you can use it. Inform your principal about your interest in using volunteers in your classroom.

3. If permitted, actively recruit volunteers: parents, community members, college students, or seniors.

4. Decide early on which tasks you will have volunteers do. If you have time early in September, hold a volunteer orientation meeting. Let them know your expectations.

5. Screen potential volunteers. Don't commit to them until you have seen them in action in the classroom. Ask yourself, "Are they good role models for students? Are they reliable? Are they available when I need them? If they are parents of children in my class, how will students react? Can volunteers be trusted with confidential information about students?" It is important that potential volunteers keep confidential any personal information about students they might observe in the classroom.

6. Make volunteers feel welcome in your class. Get them involved in class activities as soon as possible after they have expressed an interest in helping. Whenever possible, give them a regular schedule.

7. Clarify any misinterpretations or misunderstandings that may occur. Never criticize volunteers in front of individual children or the class. (This admonition applies to aides, parents, and other staff, as well.)

8. Informally monitor the work volunteers are doing. Troubleshoot when necessary. Recognize and value the work volunteers do.

See Chapter 8 for more on parent volunteers.

Specialists Who Work With the Entire Class or Grade Level

Another resource available to you may be the various specialists who work with your students. Specialists are usually adjunct staff members, including physical education, music, technology and media, art, and foreign language teachers. With today's tight finances in typical school districts, specialists must often divide their time between two or more schools. Specialists might meet with a whole class or grade level once or twice a week, or they may meet as little as once every other week. Depending on the credential status of the specialist, you may be expected to stay with your class during these sessions. If not, the time your class is with the specialist may count as your prep time. Check your school's policies and schedules for these special classes. Here are some guidelines for working with specialists:

- If your school has regularly scheduled specialists, you will receive a printed schedule of specialists serving your students. If specialists complete their own schedules, work with these teachers in planning days and times that are acceptable to you both. Record this schedule into your plan book, review the schedule with your students and their families, and post this schedule in your room.

- Whether specialists take your entire class to another area or work in your room, be sure to have your students ready on time, and be understanding if the specialist's previous class runs a few minutes late.

- Help the specialist learn the names of your students. Have your students wear nametags the first month of school. Give the specialist a printed copy of your students' pictures. Inform the specialist of any special circumstances, learning differences, or behavior issues that they need to know.
- All your students should know the rules for behavior in and out of the classroom and for working with other adults at school. Set up consistent expectations, and stick to them. (See Chapter 4 for more on discipline.)

Specialists Who Work With Individuals or Small Groups

This group of staff members includes teachers and other resource specialists who work with students in providing additional support in areas that may include reading, math, study strategies, social and behavioral support, counseling, English language development, gifted and talented programs, occupational therapy, and speech. Some of your students may be pulled out in order to meet with these professionals, although in most school districts students are required to be in their regular classes for "sacred" reading and math periods. You will be expected to work collaboratively with specialists in setting up schedules and working with students. Some specialists may work in the classroom as "push in" support, while others will have students meet outside of the classroom for "pull out" sessions. Different schools have different specialists accessible to them. Consider yourself very fortunate if your school has these professionals available. They are important resources to both your students and yourself. If you do work with them, try to meet regularly to monitor progress and goals so that you can develop consistency and work together collaboratively in and out of the classroom.

Discuss with a mentor or colleague ways to enable students to make up work they may have missed while they were out of the classroom. Think about the instruction and concepts students may have missed, rather than simply whether assignments were completed. Perhaps not all missed class work needs to be made up.

Substitute Teachers

Remember that substitute teachers are professional colleagues, too. Most substitutes are competent and well prepared, but they need your help and your students' cooperation. From time to time, remind your students how you expect them to behave for substitute teachers. The following suggestions will help your substitutes do a better job in your classroom:

- Prepare a folder for the substitute teacher ahead of time with some generic lesson plans in the event of an emergency when you may not have time to plan accordingly for the substitute. If you know you will be out, carefully plan the day with the substitute in mind. Place the sub folder with lesson plans, student nametags, and all necessary information and materials in an accessible location. Your sub folder should include

- o Detailed weekly and daily schedules, including specialist schedules, volunteers, any special events, and other specialists working with students;
- o Student names and attendance report procedures;
- o Bell schedule, recess and lunch times;
- o Emergency procedures and plans for fire and disaster drills;
- o Information about students who require special services and those who are assigned special duties;
- o Names and room numbers of helpful teachers;
- o Names of any volunteers working in the classroom;
- o Notes about school and classroom policies and procedures for discipline; and
- o Dismissal procedures and lists of children who go to after-school care, if applicable. (See Resources 1.6 and 1.7 for a sample letter and schedule and a feedback form to include in your sub folder.)

- Avoid scheduling a test or a quiz that your substitute would have to monitor.
- Avoid expecting the substitute to teach a new content area or introduce new curriculum. Avoid lessons incorporating materials or laboratory supplies that may require special procedures to use or are difficult to manage.
- Leave complete and specific instructions. The substitute may not be knowledgeable about your specific grade level or the content areas you want taught in your absence.
- Leave the names of one or two especially responsible students to assist with daily routines, operate computer or technology equipment, or answer questions.
- Leave one day's activities as a special emergency plan in case your regular lessons (e.g., a complicated writer's workshop) might be difficult for the substitute to follow. Include sufficient worksheets for your students to complete.
- Try not to be absent on Mondays and Fridays. Such absences tend to be viewed with skepticism by colleagues and administrators: "Is that teacher really ill—or just trying to extend the weekend?"
- Have a "buddy" teacher who can welcome your substitute and offer help. When you return, check with your buddy to see how effective the sub was in the classroom. This arrangement can be reciprocal.
- Remember, you do not have control over what the substitute does or does not do during the day. When you return, ask the children how the day went, and then put the day behind you, and begin anew.
- If possible, inform the children ahead of time that you will be absent, and preview the coming day's assignments. This preparation demonstrates to students your confidence and expectations that they can handle your absence cooperatively and respectfully.

KEY TERMINOLOGY AND SPECIAL PROGRAMS

Educators use many terms, acronyms, and abbreviations for various programs, characteristics, and organizations. Understanding the jargon enables you to converse with the other insiders and helps you build working relationships with them. For a list of common terms and programs, see Education Terms (Resource 1.4) and Programs for Students With Special Needs (Resource 1.5).

TAKING INITIATIVE AND REACHING OUT

Your school, like all others, is a complex social organization with its own history, culture, values, beliefs, and expectations. You will be working not only with students but also with colleagues, administrators, and parents. Although your teaching effectiveness in the classroom is important, your interactions in the professional culture of your school are crucial to surviving and flourishing in your first year and beyond.

Do not become isolated! You must consciously make time in the school day to interact professionally and personally with your colleagues. No one expects you to be perfect. You cannot have learned everything you need to know about teaching from your university preparation program, no matter how effective that program may have been. No one is ever totally prepared for the myriad day-to-day challenges of the classroom. Becoming a good teacher takes initiative, practice, and support. Yes, major challenges lie ahead. But this is an exciting time—jump in, smile, and don't forget to breathe!

RESOURCE 1.1

School Roster

You will most likely receive a school roster listing all the names, phone extensions, e-mail addresses, and emergency contact information of all the certified and classified staff at your school. Keep this list accessible, and make a copy to keep at home. Besides all the teachers, you will want to know all the other staff members.

	Phone	E-mail
Principal:		
Assistant Principal:		
Administrative Assistants:		
Custodian:		
Food Service Personnel:		
Nurse:		
Counselor/School Psychologist:		
Social Worker:		
Physical Education Teacher:		
Music/Band Teacher:		
Art Teacher:		
Library/Media Person:		
Bus Supervisors:		
Instructional Aides:		

Room Parents:	Phone	E-mail
PTA President:	Phone	E-mail
PTA Vice President:	Phone	E-mail
Speech Therapist:	Phone	E-mail
Resource Specialist:	Phone	E-mail
Special Education Teacher:	Phone	E-mail
Playground Supervisors:	Phone	E-mail

RESOURCE 1.2

School District Roster

These are district-level people you may need to contact.

Superintendent:	Phone	E-mail
Superintendent's Assistant:	Phone	E-mail
District Office Assistant:	Phone	E-mail
Business Office Manager:	Phone	E-mail
Business Services Assistant:	Phone	E-mail
Director of Facilities/Maintenance:	Phone	E-mail
School District Board of Trustees President:	Phone	E-mail
School Board Representative:	Phone	E-mail
PTA President:	Phone	E-mail
Foundation Board of Directors:	Phone	E-mail
Transportation Office:	Phone	E-mail
Substitute Number:	Phone	E-mail

RESOURCE 1.3

School Information Checklist

Here are some important questions to have answered by your school principal before school begins, if they have not already been addressed during new teacher work days:

_____ 1. How do I get the keys to my classroom or other rooms to which I may need access?

_____ 2. If necessary furniture is not in my room, how can I get additional tables, student desks, and so on?

_____ 3. Will I be working with any students with special needs? English language learners, physically impaired, or resource students? Do they, or any other students, leave my room during the day? If so, what are their schedules, and how can I familiarize myself with their cum files? Can I meet with them and their families before school begins? Do any of my students have special needs that require accommodations in my room arrangement or instructional methods?

_____ 4. Will an instructional aide be assigned to work with me and, if so, what is the schedule?

_____ 5. What are the school rules and policies I will need to present to students?

_____ 6. What are the procedures for obtaining classroom books, supplies, and materials and for issuing them to students?

_____ 7. What expendable supplies are available, and what are the procedures for obtaining them?

_____ 8. What media and technology tools are available for me and my students to have access to, and what are the procedures for obtaining them?

_____ 9. What is the procedure for the arrival of students, recording attendance, and dismissal on the first day of school and for every day after that? (See also numbers 13 and 17.)

_____10. What will my specialist schedule look like?

_____11. How do students leave at the end of the day? Do I have any bus riders? Do I have children going to day care or other activities on or off campus I need to be aware of?

_____12. What policies do I need to be aware of, and how do I get assistance from the office for emergencies, illness, or discipline problems?

_____13. What are the office procedures for early dismissal and late arrivals?

_____14. Is a school nurse available? What are appropriate reasons for making a referral?

_____15. Is a counselor or school psychologist available? What types of referrals does she want?

_____16. What district resources are available for support in working with students with learning or behavior problems?

_____17. What custodial services are available for my room, and what should I do if there is an emergency cleanup need?

_____18. To what parts of the building may I send students (library, restroom, etc.), and what procedures do I follow to send them?

_____19. What is the bell schedule? (Are there bells?)

_____20. How can I get a district and school calendar and roster?

_____21. Where are student cum files kept? What are the procedures to access them?

_____22. Will I be assigned a mentor or a buddy teacher? Will I participate in a new-teacher induction program?

_____23. What is the policy for visitors to sign in before coming on campus?

_____24. When are you (the principal) available, and for what purposes should I be certain to consult with you?

_____25. Are there any special events or assemblies I need to be aware of in the first weeks of school?

RESOURCE 1.4

Education Terms

4th Friday Count	Attendance records on which state aid is based in some states
ACT	American College of Testing
ADA	Average daily attendance—a count of students in attendance, on which state funding amounts are based
ADD	Attention deficit disorder
ADHD	Attention deficit hyperactivity disorder
(___) AEYC	(State) Association for the Education of Young Children
AFT	American Federation of Teachers
AI	Autistically impaired
(___) ASCD	(State) Association for Supervision and Curriculum Development
ASCD	Association for Supervision and Curriculum Development
At-Risk	Students who are low achieving because of a number of factors
CAT	California Achievement Test
CTBS	Comprehensive Tests of Basic Skills
(___) CTM	(State) Council of Teachers of Mathematics
Cum files	Cumulative records for students
(___) EA	(State) Education Association
(___) EAP	(State) Education Assessment Program
EBD	Emotional-behavior disorder
ECE	Early childhood education
EDY	Educationally disadvantaged youth
EI	Emotionally impaired
ELD	English language development
ELL	English language learner
EMI	Emotionally and mentally impaired
ERIC	Educational Resource Information Center
ESD	Educational Service District
ESEA	Elementary and Secondary Education Act of 1988, which provides funds to districts to meet needs of EDY
ESL	English as a second language
FEP	Fluent English proficient
GATE	Gifted and talented education

(Continued)

(Continued)

HI	Hearing impaired
IEP	Individualized education plan
IRA	International Reading Association
ISD	Intermediate school district
IT	Technology support
ITBS	Iowa Tests of Basic Skills
ITIP	Instructional theory into practice
LD	Learning disabled
LEP	Limited English proficient
LRE	Least restrictive environment
LS	Learning specialist
NAEYC	National Association for the Education of Young Children
NCLB	No Child Left Behind Act
NCSS	National Council of Social Studies
NCTE	National Council of Teachers of English
NCTM	National Council of Teachers of Mathematics
NEA	National Education Association
NEP	Non-English proficient
Para-Pro	Paraprofessional
PET	Parent effectiveness training
PLC	Professional learning communities
POHI	Physically and otherwise health impaired
(__) RA	(State) Reading Association
RTI	Response to intervention
SAT	Scholastic Aptitude Test
SCE	State Compensatory Education
SPED ED	Special education
SST	Student study team
TBS	Test of Basic Skills
TC	Teacher consultant
TET	Teacher effectiveness training
VI	Visually impaired

RESOURCE 1.5

Programs for Students With Special Needs

Students with specific educational needs have the opportunity to participate in specifically funded programs. These programs are designed to provide additional assistance for identified students. Some of the specifically funded projects that may be available at your school site are included here.

Title I

Students who score below the 40th percentile in reading and/or mathematics on a standardized achievement test such as the Comprehensive Tests of Basic Skills (CTBS) are identified as educationally disadvantaged youth (EDY). EDY is a federal designation for students whose educational attainment is below the level appropriate for their age made on the basis of a nationally norm-referenced test. If your school is a Title I school, identified students are eligible to receive extra help in reading, mathematics, and language arts. Federal funds are allocated for this purpose. How students receive this service varies.

State Compensatory Education

State Compensatory Education (SCE) funds are allocated by most states to provide extra service and support for students who fall below the 40th percentile on standardized achievement tests.

Limited English Proficient/Title VII

Some students are identified as limited English proficient (LEP) or non-English proficient (NEP). Federal funds are allocated for the purpose of providing extra service and support for these students until they reach the level of fluent English proficient (FEP).

Special Education Programs

Students who are eligible for special education programs have been referred, identified, assessed, and placed in the most suitable programs. Individualized education plans (IEPs) will recommend the extent to which such students should be mainstreamed into regular classrooms. Placement follows the convention of the least restrictive environment (LRE).

Gifted and Talented Education Program

Students in gifted and talented education (GATE) programs are provided supplementary services that usually include an emphasis on reasoning skills, creative problem solving, and evaluative thinking. Some gifted and talented programs also address spatial intelligences and artistic and leadership abilities. A variety of teaching styles and materials are used to support and challenge students while developing their abilities.

RESOURCE 1.6

Sample Cover Letter for a Substitute Folder

Date

Dear (substitute's name if you know it) Substitute:

I've prepared the information in this folder to provide you with a good deal of general information about my class and schedule. Whenever possible, I'll furnish specific daily lesson plans in addition to the enclosed materials. I hope this folder is useful and that you have a good day with my group.

Instructional aide: _____ Times: _____

Student helpers:_____

Parent volunteers: _____

Specialists:_____

Special event/activities/project: _____

Office number: _____

Teacher next door if you need assistance: _____

When you finish the day, please complete the feedback sheet, and return it to the office with the folder. Thanks for your help.

Sincerely,

Teacher: _____ Room: _____ Grade: _____

Home phone number: _____

Inside this folder you will find:

- Attendance forms
- Building and playground rules
- Class list
- Classroom rules
- Emergency procedures
- Feedback form for you to fill out
- Groups for centers activities
- Lesson plans for centers activities
- Lists of allergies and special needs
- Schedules (classroom and building)
- Seating chart
- Student name tags
- Students' family contact information
- Time schedule

Time Schedule	Routine
Students arrive at	
School begins at	
Recess is scheduled for	
Lunch time is	
Noon recess is	
Dismissal time is	
Specialist schedule	

RESOURCE 1.7

Feedback Form for a Substitute Folder

From Your Substitute

Name: _____ Date: _____ Class: _____

The day went . . .

The lesson plans and instruction . . .

The students were . . .

Students who were absent, tardy, or out of class

Any problems . . .

Comments . . .

2

Organizing Your Classroom and Yourself

WHAT TO DO AND THINK ABOUT BEFORE THE STUDENTS ARRIVE

A welcoming, well-organized classroom motivates students and augments your instruction. It sends the message to students and their families that you are professional, well organized, and that you are planning an exciting year. Your classroom is a reflection of you in many ways. It demonstrates what you consider important in the classroom. How will you transform stark walls and blank bulletin boards into an engaging and effective learning environment? Ponder the physical design of the room as well as class routines, procedures, and groupings. List all your great ideas for the coming year. Then, to be realistic, eliminate 50 percent of them! Circle the key remaining items that truly resonate with you, and start with these. Ideas for which you feel a passion are the easiest to implement.

Function is the most important aspect of any classroom environment. A well-organized room not only keeps materials ordered and accessible to students but also allows for a variety of learning styles and learning situations. As you arrange your room, decide where groups will meet, where supplies will be kept, and how you and the students will move around the classroom. Clarify that mental image of what you want your classroom to be like. What is the feeling? How does it look (ordered or relaxed)? Are students' supplies, your teaching materials, books, and technology tools accessible? How will students move around the classroom? What will the flow of traffic look like? Will every student be able to learn to their maximum potential here? How can you design the room so that students will be proud of it and take ownership for it? Survey and note any repair needs and report them immediately to the office. Request additional furniture or adjustments in desk heights to meet students' needs, and request help moving furniture. Protect your back! Get help, and don't try to do it all alone. Look at other classrooms, and get ideas from other teachers. Take a deep breath, and enjoy the excitement of the new school year.

SETTING UP YOUR CLASSROOM

To make your classroom a positive environment for learning, make sure that all necessary items are in place before the children arrive.

Physical Equipment

- Enough desks or tables with chairs for each student
- Teacher desk and additional table for instructional aides and/or parent volunteers
- Teacher and additional adult chairs
- Large tables for science experiments and group projects
- Storage space for students' personal belongings (coats, backpacks, lunches, etc.): cubbies, hooks, and/or shelves
- Storage space for supplies: shelves, filing cabinets, storage containers, or boxes (labeled so you know what is inside)
- Table and chairs for meetings of small instructional groups
- Pencil sharpeners, trash cans, recycling bins, clock
- Electrical outlets, extension cords, surge protectors, projection screen or Smartboard, technology cart, AVerVision or projector
- Reading corner with furniture and/or beanbag chairs or pillows
- Listening center (with books and tapes)
- World and U.S. maps
- Large mounted whiteboard
- Student technology area: computers or desktops
- Drinking water

Supplies

- Lesson plan book
- Grade book and attendance register (if attendance is not done online)
- Teacher instructional manuals, student workbooks, and instructional supplies
- Sets of texts or instructional materials for each content area you will teach and related teacher guides
- Reference books, maps, charts, globe, calendar, number line, and alphabet (manuscript display or cursive)
- Student set of whiteboards (with dry erase pens, and erasers), pencils, erasers, crayons, colored pencils, colored markers (including multiracial skin colors), watercolors, tempura paint, rulers, scissors, paper, tape, glue sticks, glue, Sharpies, and staplers

- Reading easel (for Big Books), classroom library books, and magazines
- Art paper and painting easel
- Math manipulatives and science materials
- Dramatic play and building blocks (for younger students)
- Cleaning supplies (keep these out of reach of students, and use "green," nonpolluting varieties), paper towels, hand soap, hand sanitizer, dustpan, and broom
- Personal items (hairbrush, toothbrush, toothpaste, ibuprofen, energy bars, etc.)
- Set of emergency change of clothes (slacks, shirt, sweater, shoes, and socks)
- Miscellaneous supplies (e.g., newspapers, old shirts for art projects, kitchen gloves, cooking utensils, apron, plastic recycled food containers, dish soap, sponges, and old towels and rags)

TEACHING TIPS

Be familiar with any student supplies list that may have been sent home prior to the start of school before you begin to calculate if you have enough supplies.

Keep cleaning materials, personal items, and student files locked away inside file cabinets. Anything confidential that you would not want a parent or older student to see should be filed away from easy access.

For ease of supplies handling, you can assign a student "supplies coordinator" for each table group or desk grouping (if you arrange desks in a cluster). Fill a basket of supplies (scissors, markers, rulers, glue, staplers, etc.) for each table group. Leave labeled baskets on a special shelf to be picked up when needed. Then, ask supplies coordinators to get and return baskets for their tables.

Keep clutter to a minimum. For many students, clutter provides a distraction. Organization and clear working space helps many students stay focused on their work.

Stay on top of the organization. Take a few minutes each day to return things (supplies, books, materials, files, etc.) to their proper place. Otherwise, at the end of the year you will be faced with an enormous filing job. In addition, students will know that everything has a place. They will not have the excuse that they don't know where something is or that their work "got lost" in the classroom!

Organizing Room Space

Consider how you will deliver instruction and how students will work. The seating arrangement you choose will reflect your teaching. Will students be working in whole groups, small groups, in partners, triads, or individually? Do you plan to begin the year with students sitting in rows, in a U shape, or in clusters? Arrange the desks or tables accordingly. (See the Desk Placement section later in this chapter.) As the year progresses, change these seating arrangements to suit the needs of your students and of the instructional activities. *Be flexible!* For example, you may add an additional learning center or put student desks in a U shape for oral sharing of completed projects. When you are ready to have your students participate in a whole-class dramatic activity, Reader's Theatre, or a class presentation, you can always move aside desks to accommodate the amount of space needed for a given activity. You may also decide at some point during the year to try a different seating arrangement. Your students will most likely think the change is exciting! Remember to have wheelchair accessibility in your room. You may have students or family members who will need additional space to accommodate their special needs.

Consider how you will provide room for one or more students who are unable to cope behaviorally or academically in class. These pupils may at times work better alone or with a partner. Seat students who are easily distracted near the front of the room to minimize distractions and help them to stay focused. Find out from the previous year's teachers which students will most likely need to be separated from each other.

Do you have room for a rug? Especially if you teach primary children, set aside an open space for a large rug or carpet on which children can sit in a semicircle for calendar and morning meeting activities, language arts, and whole-group instructional time.

Consider how your use of technology will impact the seating arrangement. Do you have a Smartboard students need to see and participate with? Will you have students who are visually or hearing impaired that will need seating accommodations?

Especially for primary-age children, provide a place for creative play. Supply this area with costumes for dressing up (no hats because of the risk of spreading head lice), construction tools, play cooking utensils, plastic food, phones, calculators, pads of paper, menus, and shopping lists. Encourage creativity, role-playing, communication skills, conflict resolution, social interaction, and literacy simultaneously! If your room is small, and you must choose between a library corner and a space for dramatics, opt for the library corner.

Providing a well-stocked library corner (including children's magazines, fiction, nonfiction, library books, and student-authored books) is inviting to children and is a wonderful place for children to spend quiet moments alone.

Provide a writing center. Supply paper, scissors, pencils, erasers, colored markers and pencils, crayons, staplers, and glue sticks. Place the area near the word wall if at all possible in a primary classroom, so students have access to words they need help spelling. Encourage students to make books, cards, and to write letters.

For young primary students, provide a construction building area if space permits. You will need unit blocks, Lego sets, Lincoln Logs, or other building materials appropriate for your grade level. An art area with easel and paints, watercolors, glue, scissors, paper, and fabric scraps encourages creativity and fine motor skills.

Consider a permanent listening center with tape player, earphones, and recorded books—fiction and nonfiction. Audiocassette stories provide excellent read-aloud models for children gaining reading fluency. Look into software you can download on the student computers for read alouds, as well. There are some very good programs available for students to read along with the text and enjoy the illustrations.

If you have classroom computers, be sure to plan for how you will be using them in your classroom. Will all students have use of a computer? Will they be accessible at all times? Will they be used for writing? What will your system be for students using the computers? Or, will your class be visiting a computer lab with or without tech support?

Creating a Classroom Library

Every classroom needs a collection of books. The classroom library is essential. The classroom library is your most powerful tool for convincing children that you value reading. Even if you teach in a school with a wonderful central library and media center, your classroom should have an attractive collection of paperbacks and hardbacks that invites browsing and reading. The collection of class books needs to serve many purposes. One purpose is to supply leveled books for emergent and early readers. You will need books at different levels for students' varying abilities during sustained silent reading (SSR). You will need books for browsing. These will be both fiction and nonfiction. Consider books that represent diversity. This includes differences in ethnicity, culture, race, economic status, gender, sexual preference, disabilities, and family structure. Choose books that represent a wide range of subjects, including respecting differences, exploring different characters and roles, conflict resolution, and problem solving. Choose books in different genres, include classics, and include stories with contemporary themes. Choose high-interest books and books that supplement teaching units. Most of all, create a library corner that everyone uses and enjoys and meets a wide variety of interests.

Depending on your personality, you may want to allow students to read on a rug, pillows, an upholstered chair or couch, or other "homey" furniture in the library corner. In any case, make sure the reading area is inviting. Send e-mails to publishers to ask for their bright, fun, free materials—posters, bookmarks, and so forth. Use book jackets on bulletin boards. Staple up children's drawings inspired by books. Yes, it takes time to fill empty bookshelves. Start now! One way to get going is to ask your students if they have books at home that they are willing to share for the year. Check garage sales, thrift shops, used book stores, and online sites (Amazon is one—look under "children's books" for used titles). Enroll your class in a book club (Scholastic is a good one), and get free class books with your bonus points. If your school has an annual book fair—as many do—teachers can provide wish lists to be posted at the sale for any families who would like to purchase a book to donate. Start a "Birthday Book" program in which the birthday child brings a favorite book as a gift for the class. Inscribe that book with the child's name and birthday. Many school districts and PTAs give beginning teachers a stipend for purchasing supplementary materials—an excellent way to fund a core of classroom library books. Don't forget to use both your school and public library as excellent resources for borrowing books. Be persistent, and over time you'll build a classroom collection with hundreds of titles and the types of books you want.

See Resources 2.2 through 2.3 for suggestions on how to introduce library corner rules, book checkout procedures, and record keeping.

SUGGESTED MATERIALS FOR THE CLASSROOM LIBRARY

- Open-faced bookshelves
- A rug or carpet section
- Pillows
- A rocking chair
- Beanbag chairs
- Table and chairs
- Special quiet places for reading
- Plastic baskets or tubs of books labeled by author, series, theme, topic, or genre (animals, humor, fantasy, fables, history, biography, concept books, poetry, riddles, etc.)
- Plastic tubs or baskets of high-quality magazines for children (e.g., *Zoobooks, Cobblestone, Cricket, Sports Illustrated Kids, Highlights*)
- For kindergarten and first grade, Big Books used previously in shared reading
- Plastic tub or basket labeled "Books Our Class Has Written"

Bulletin Boards

Bulletin boards in today's classrooms reflect student learning. They are a showcase for student work. If possible, have bulletin boards and display areas clear and ready before school starts. If you need bulletin board ideas, ask to look at other classrooms around your school. Plan on some early projects that you can hang soon after school has begun to fill the bulletin boards. Backgrounds for bulletin boards may be done with neutral colors, fadeless paper, fabric, or wallpaper. Take a photo of your bulletin boards for your portfolio and for future reference.

One bulletin board you will need to prepare for the first day of school will be the calendar and daily schedule. A number line and alphabet (manuscript and/or cursive) are also important. You may want to include a weather chart and the number of school days. Classroom rules and consequences can be posted once they are discussed and decided upon with the class.

Include student work from a wide variety of subjects. Include a self-portrait at the beginning of the year. Consider a technology piece and writing samples about the beginning of school or a summer experience. Include scientific observations and math representations. A timesaving tip for the busy teacher is to use permanent bulletin board captions, such as "Student of the Week," "Quote of the Week," and "Word of the Week." You might include birthdays, lost teeth, baby pictures ("guess who"), and seasonal projects.

Remember: Prior to posting any photographs of students in the classroom, on class or school websites, or in local papers, you will need the written permission of the child's family. Parents may wish to not have their child's picture in any of these publicly viewed places.

Desk Placement

One of the biggest decisions that most teachers (veterans as well as beginners) make at the start of each school year relates to furniture arrangement. How you arrange your desks is dependent on not only your teaching style but also on how you accommodate technology in your classroom. Start by doing an inventory of the number and also the type of seats, desks, and tables available. Several large tables are handy for meeting with small groups or setting up activity centers. In primary classrooms, a curved reading table is especially useful.

An important next step is to reflect on your personal educational philosophy and style of teaching. How often will you use small-group or cooperative-learning activities? Will you set up centers? Depending on the space available, you may use several types of arrangements concurrently. For instance, you may set up several learning centers for students to work alone or in small groups, a carpet in one area for students to gather on the floor, and a corner with a table and chairs to accommodate small learning groups. Do you have corrals that can be put out on desks for students to do more independent, "private" work and test taking? Decide how to seat students in order for them to access the ways in which you incorporate technology into your instruction.

Seating groups or clusters of three to five are increasingly common in elementary classrooms (Figure 2.1). Cluster arrangements are useful for group discussions, cooperative learning, and various small-group assignments.

Figure 2.1 Group Seating Arrangements

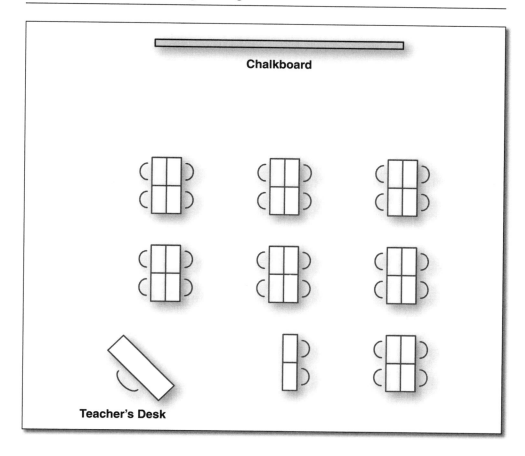

Before the opening day, review your class roster with your mentor, or check with the prior year's teachers, to determine a successful seating arrangement. Find out ahead of time if there are students who are easily distracted, who your English language learners are, and if you have students that should not be sitting together. Find out if there is a student who should be sitting near another, particular student. Check student files carefully, so you know the students before school begins.

Be cognizant of the makeup of each cluster. Consider the emotional, behavioral, cognitive needs, and gender of each student in the cluster. Consider English language learners, students with disabilities, and those students who are especially talkative and those who may be very quiet. Integrate sexes, abilities, and racial and cultural groups. Try different combinations of students.

As you consider flexibility in seating arrangements, think carefully about how you will prepare students for movement and transitions between groups or activities. Each arrangement has its own rules and procedures. Regardless of what seating arrangement you use, always keep a seating chart in your plan book in case a substitute needs to take over your class. *Be flexible:* Seating arrangements can easily be changed as frequently as you see fit.

Place nametags on each desk before students arrive.

Obtaining Teacher Manuals and Materials

Teacher editions of student textbooks will never substitute for your own specific planning, but they make the process immensely easier for your beginning year. Using the teacher guide does not negate your personal convictions and skills or your knowledge of your students' differences, interests, and abilities. Your final decisions about what to teach are guided by all of these.

Make sure, at the least, that you start the school year with reference copies of the basic teacher guide for each text or instructional program you will use with your students. In most schools, teacher manuals accompany each classroom set of student textbooks that are issued to you. Textbook publishers provide extensive teaching suggestions in the teacher guides as well as resource materials to help you extend the learning beyond the student text.

You have probably discovered that many teacher editions are accompanied by sequentially designed resource units from which you can select and build specific lessons and teaching units. Typically, a resource unit consists of a comprehensive list of objectives, a large number and variety of activities, suggested materials, links to websites, extensive bibliographies, suggestions for integrating the units in other subject areas, and information on how the lessons meet state content standards.

Sometimes, a beginning teacher asks, "How closely must I follow the school's or school district's curriculum guide or the course of study outlined in the officially adopted textbooks?" The answer to this important question varies widely. You may not wish to follow the guide exactly or use all its many suggestions. Certainly, you will want an answer before you start teaching. Discuss this with your principal, mentor, grade-level coordinator, or grade-level team. Some schools want curriculum closely followed, and some want it scripted. Some schools allow for flexibility in individual pacing and content inclusion, while others want the grade level to be more closely aligned and on the same topic and schedule for each unit.

Additional support materials are available from the publishers of most textbook series or units. These components include:

- Blackline masters of practice materials and worksheets;
- Student workbooks, kits, charts, audiocassettes, CDs or videos, and Big Books;
- Overhead transparencies or computer software;
- Math manipulatives or science materials; and
- Diagnostic and assessment materials.

Look at the publisher's website. Everything is available online. Also, check for what is included at no cost and what "consumable" materials your school may already have or will purchase.

Using the Teacher Manuals

Most teacher editions of textbooks provide a reduced version of the student text reproduced along with answers and related notes. Accompanying this material are suggestions for presenting, implementing, and enriching each lesson. For science units, manuals provide background information to help build upon prior knowledge before starting a new unit.

Teacher guides may not include material you want to use or enough variety to accommodate the various abilities of your students. Expect this to happen. Sometimes, you will be able to modify this material to suit your particular needs and to differentiate instruction in order to meet students' needs by extending the lessons or by simplifying them.

Setting Up a Literacy-Rich Classroom

Reading and writing: If you are planning an effective language arts program for emerging readers, you need to design a "print-rich" classroom environment. Print-rich classrooms immerse children in an environment that serves as a ready reference for understanding written language and conveying meaning. For instance, one suggestion for kindergarten and first-grade classes is to label the classroom fixtures, furniture, and objects. The goal is to make your classroom full of print. Songs, poems, jokes, riddles, recipes, and group writing should be enlarged and written on charts. Place these charts around the room for children to read alone or with peers. Classroom walls can be covered with many lists. Post the daily schedule, calendar, lunch menu, and classroom helpers and their jobs. Write out displays of classroom rules, directions for use of centers, activities directions, sign-up boards for conferences, and all management schemes. Display sight words, blends, diagraphs, and examples of conventions of print for students to consult during writing. Include magnetic letters, scissors, rulers, and rubber stamps of letters, pencils, and markers. And, of course, you will want many, many books!

Encourage writing with a fun writing center where children are free to make books, write stories, write cards and letters, and illustrate their work. Model good writing each day during a morning message and in mini-lessons in writer's workshop with the AVerVision. Read aloud each day to encourage a love of reading and good literacy conversations, or "book talk" about literature. In kindergarten and first-grade classes, set up a mail center, so students can write letters to their classmates. Cut up pictures from calendars, and have students write stories about the pictures. Encourage students to make up their own stories and create their own books.

Speaking and Listening

Create many opportunities for students to practice speaking and listening skills, part of their language arts development. Community circle, class meetings, student of the week, and daily helper offer opportunities for students to speak in front of their peers. Listening to other students as well as to the teacher and following multistep directions provides good listening-skill practice.

Setting Up a Literacy-Rich Classroom for Emerging Readers

Materials You Will Need

- Lots of books—hundreds—and many different kinds of books!
- Lots of magazines—high interest and those specifically related to student interest, science, geography, sports, or literacy
- Two or three pocket charts (vinyl, see-through pocket charts are recommended; these charts can be ordered from most school supply stores or catalogs)
- Lots of blank sentence strips and word cards
- Sufficient number of black felt-tip pens for all your students
- Sheets of chart paper or a roll of butcher paper
- Overhead projector, screen, and blank transparencies, or AVerVision, and Smartboard

EXAMPLES OF LITERACY-RICH ACTIVITIES

- Every day, read to the children, usually from a chapter book. Read a book that you enjoy and that challenges the students to listen. Demand their attention, and check for comprehension.
- Every day, have sustained silent reading (SSR).
- Every day, sing a song or chant a familiar poem (which might include something patriotic like the Pledge of Allegiance).
- Every day, have the children write.
- Every day, make sure that the students have time for individual or small-group work in which they read and write without your direct instruction.

FINDING TIME AND BALANCE IN YOUR PERSONAL AND PROFESSIONAL LIFE

As you begin your teaching career, you will find that you have more things to do and more details to remember than ever before. There are increasingly more and more demands on teachers. You have so many responsibilities. At times, it seems overwhelming, and it appears that there is simply not enough time in the day to get everything done. Paperwork, planning, filing, organizing, meetings, and keeping up with e-mails take more and more of a teacher's time each day. So, how do you find the time and balance that you need?

Using time well is a key to enhancing your effectiveness. Focus on the *really* important activities by clarifying your priorities. *Prioritize.* Decide which tasks must be done right away and which can be completed at a later time. Mark all tasks, deadlines, events, meetings, conferences, and important dates in your plan book, along with times and dates of present and future commitments. Break especially large or difficult jobs into manageable pieces, and start making progress right away. Use markers or brightly colored ink to color code and remind you of priorities and deadlines. (See Resource 2.1 for help with To Do lists).

A teacher's life is filled with forms, evaluations, notices, student papers, report cards, progress reports, planning, cumulative record files, memos, staff and grade-level meetings, committee work, meeting with parents, IEPs, letters, e-mail, reading material, lesson plans, and files of curriculum materials and instructional activities. Unless you develop effective ways of reducing the paperwork load and keeping it from hampering your overall performance, you will soon fall behind. You will find yourself faced for the most part with two types of school paperwork tasks:

1. Those tasks that are not directly related to teaching, for example, district forms, cumulative record cards, memos, and meeting agendas and minutes

2. Those tasks that are related to your classroom and teaching, for example, lesson planning, grading, and recording

To organize more efficiently, consider keeping separate folders for different types of paperwork, such as student papers and office notices. Label each folder.

Huge stacks of student papers to correct can be overwhelming. Student work must be corrected quickly, recorded, and passed back to your students. Feedback is important to students, and you need to monitor their progress.

Have your students correct as much of their own work as possible in class as part of whole-group instruction. Many teachers set up a file crate box with hanging files and folders for each student. Throughout the week, after students have reviewed their corrected papers, they are filed in the proper folder. On Friday, all the week's work is sent home to parents in a Friday folder, usually with the class newsletter (see Chapter 7) and any memoranda from the office. This efficient, once-a-week system is well organized, saves time for busy teachers, and keeps parents up to date on their child's progress.

Use parents' help. You may be reluctant to ask for such help, feeling that you should be able to do it all and not impose on parents. Yet, many parents are pleased to help prepare work, file, fill folders, make copies, cut out templates, or help hang work on classroom bulletin boards. Just be mindful of what you give parents to do. Do not give them work or tests that they probably should not be seeing.

Build responsibility! Use your students to provide regular assistance in keeping the room cleaned and organized, counting out and distributing certain materials, and doing other routine chores. All children need to be taught to clean up after themselves. Remember that distributing papers is a coveted task that may be reserved for elected monitors or rotated so that everyone gets a turn.

Establish your own personal goals and priorities. It is easy to allow professional priorities to eat up much of your personal time. Set limits for yourself, so you efficiently get done what you need to, but save some time for yourself and your personal and family needs. You will be a better teacher if you make time for yourself, enjoy quality time away from the classroom, and find the balance in your personal and professional life.

Set Priorities and Find Shortcuts

1. List the routine things you need to do—plan, correct papers, record grades, put up bulletin boards, file materials, make copies, download pictures, and so forth.

2. Look at the time you have available: before and after school and during music, physical education, and library time (if you are lucky to have these breaks in your day). Consider how you spend your time before and after work. Try to use this time effectively. Find additional time by jotting down lesson and activity ideas from your present lessons for future use. Keep your ideas in your plan book to refer to for next year. This way, you will not have to reinvent the wheel. Consider planning and prepping materials with other members of your team. When you are done with a unit, take the extra time to put things back where they belong so that they are organized for your use next year.

3. Use other teachers' ideas (OTIs). Listen to other teachers. You may hear something that will work for you. Better yet, ask other teachers, including your mentor, how they find time to do things.

4. Decide if the time spent looking for a certain book or resource is worthwhile. Perhaps an alternative would be even more effective.

5. Consider outside factors (e.g., the copy machine is always crowded in the morning but not during your prep period; parents come to visit unannounced; too many e-mails). What can you do to minimize these? Watch out for typical time wasters (excessive chatting with your teacher aide, errands, getting coffee, trips to the school office or supply closet, idle telephone conversations, a cluttered desk, inadequate filing system, inability to say no, etc.).

6. Write a prioritized To Do list containing what must be done first, second, third, and so on. See Resource 2.1 for a handy list format and additional ideas.

7. Plan ahead for times that will involve extra work (e.g., before progress reports, parent-teacher conferences, back-to-school night, and open house). Don't procrastinate.

8. Use all those good classroom management ideas you have learned to organize your room and your routines so that, as a whole, your classroom runs smoothly.

9. Avoid taking on anything extra unless the reasons for taking it on balance out the time that is involved.

Sources of Stress

As a beginning teacher, expect to experience some stress. Following are common sources of stress frequently cited by teachers:

- Difficult students
- Difficult parents of students
- Loneliness and isolation from other teachers
- Too little time and too much to do
- Managing the classroom and instruction
- Dealing with paperwork and e-mails
- Coping with the workload: planning instruction for at least five subject areas, teaching outside your area of expertise, and too many extracurricular responsibilities
- Expectations and demands from your administrator
- Self: allowing work to pile up; conflict or problems with parents, administrators, colleagues, or students

Adjusting to the work environment found in a typical elementary school is not easy, particularly when reality shock first sets in. Stress can become a problem if you let it. For some, a little stress can be positive, keeping you on your toes. Don't let stress become overwhelming, thus increasing your fatigue and limiting your productivity and effectiveness.

Tips for Relieving Stress

Every situation has its own set of stressors. Sit down and figure out what things cause you stress. Identify those things that you can control, and then work to minimize the stress involved. If stress is caused by some things you cannot control, find a way to manage them. Try managing your time optimally by setting a timeline and creating your own deadlines for getting work accomplished. Use stress-management techniques such as meditation or other relaxation methods, deep muscle massage, exercise, enjoyable time with friends, and a healthy diet. Explore alternatives to help minimize stress and to deal with it in ways that fit your lifestyle. Throughout the process, focus on your strengths and celebrate and share your successes. Here are some ways to handle different types of stress.

School Stress

Begin with aspects you can control, such as how you manage your classroom and relate to students. If work feels dull, for example, break your routine. If you teach young children, take time to play and interact with them. Older children might enjoy a new art or science project or a backward schedule, in which you reverse the usual sequence of activities.

While you are at it, take another look at your classroom's physical appearance, such as bulletin boards and the arrangement of desks and other furniture. Evaluate what you *have* to do versus what you think you *should* do. Maybe you really don't have to change the bulletin board or reorganize the book collections yet. At the same time, renewing the landscape of the room might give you a lift and revitalize you *and* your students.

Remember your students. Make sure that your expectations for them are realistic and clear. Sometimes, stress is caused by pushing to "cover" (rather than *teach*) all the required curriculum for your grade level. You might need to slow down to meet your students' needs. Be aware of stress your students might be feeling, as well. Discuss with your mentor or principal covering the curriculum scope and sequence while differentiating instruction realistically for each student's needs.

Have you also set realistic expectations and allowed a few minutes for yourself? Do you stretch, relax, and breathe deeply from time to time during the day? Try stretching, relaxing, and some yoga with your students. They will appreciate it, too!

Personal Stress

Much of the stress you experience is the result of coping with the demands of a busy schedule at school and home. Some teachers do all the day's paperwork at school, and enjoy some free, unstructured time at home. Other teachers leave school when the contract school day is over and instead finish up in the quiet and comfort of their homes. Once you leave school, how do you spend your time? Do you make time for yourself? Can you take some time to walk, run, go to the gym, and meet a friend for a coffee? Are you running around, driving children to and from activities, making dinner, or running errands? We all have different commitments and personal priorities. Whatever they are, try to fit some special time in for yourself. You will be pleasantly surprised at how good you will feel! You will be more productive in school as well.

RESOURCE 2.1

Time Management for
the Busy Teacher: Your To Do List

As a successful beginning teacher, you are doing careful and complete lesson planning.

Successful time managers organize their in-school activities in a thoughtful, systematic manner. Start by clarifying your objectives. Exactly what do you need to get accomplished? Use your plan book or iCal to look at the overall year. Your plan book or calendar will help you to stay organized. Plan in your teaching units with your team. Plan the quarter, the month, the week, and each day. Plan in parent conferences, open house, back-to-school night, other school events, vacations, teacher workdays, and holidays. Plan in your assessment and testing periods, field trips, parent volunteers, progress reports, homework, and class projects. Then, ask yourself what activities must take place to achieve your objectives by the end of the week. After you identify activities, set priorities, and estimate the time needed to complete each one of them. Many busy teachers find it useful to spend a few minutes at the end of each day preparing a daily To Do list for the coming day. Keep focused on the big picture as well as on your personal objectives and priorities for each day. Use a To Do list if it will help you stay organized. (See the following sample.)

Make sure you do some personal planning for the other important activities in your life. You may feel you don't have enough time to plan, but you won't have any more time available for your activities until you *do* plan effectively!

DAILY TO DO LIST

Date: _____

Item	Priority	Done	Scheduled Events	
			7:00	
			8:00	
			9:00	
			10:00	
			11:00	
			12:00	
			1:00	
			2:00	
			3:00	
Notes				
			4:00	
			5:00	
			6:00	
			7:00	
			8:00	

RESOURCE 2.2

Library Corner Introduction:
Sample Lesson Plan

Introduction to the Classroom Library

Objectives

- To introduce materials in the library corner
- To establish rules for the use of the library corner

Materials

- See the box, Suggested Materials for the Classroom Library, page 32

Step-By-Step Plan

1. Bring children into the classroom library. Ask them to sit on the rug. Explain that they will have a daily opportunity to use the many books and materials available. Discuss when during the day they may come to the library corner (e.g., after their guided reading group, after they have completed other assignments, during independent reading time, and perhaps during recess or lunch).

2. Show and discuss the variety of materials they can use during classroom library time. Explain that they can work alone or with others. Buddy reading in quiet voices is OK.

3. Discuss and demonstrate the following rules:
   - Handle books and materials carefully.
   - Select only one item at a time.
   - Put a completed book away in the proper place (bookshelf or tub) before selecting another.
   - Treat each other with courtesy and respect.

4. Allow time for students to explore the books and audio books. If necessary, assist children in looking for "just right" books. Be prepared to closely supervise children's use of the library corner during the first week. When the class has mastered selecting and checking out books, introduce the idea of independent reading at a specific time each day, and explain how to keep a record of books read.

RESOURCE 2.3

Introduction to Checking Out Books:
Sample Lesson Plan for a Checkout System

How to Check Books Out of the Classroom Library

Objectives

- To explain the system for checking books out and back into the classroom library
- To encourage reading at home

Materials

- Large zip-lock bag, laminated manila folder or plastic "book bag" for each student, with student name, class number, and school written on front
- Colored 8" by 10" tag board form to record books sent home with the date and a check-off column for when books get returned to be kept inside book bag

Step-by-Step Plan

1. Bring children into the classroom library. Ask them to sit on the rug. Review rules about the use of the classroom library and the location of materials in it (ask, "Who can show us where the tub of fantasy books is?" "Humor?" "Harry Potter?" etc.).

2. Explain that books can be checked out of the classroom library to be read at home. Show the book bags. Explain and demonstrate the procedures for checking books out and returning them.

   a. To check a book out, children take the colored tag board form in their book bag, write the title on it, and make sure they have returned all other books first before checking out new ones.

   b. To check the book back in when it is returned, children take the tag board form from their book bag, write the date they're returning it and a short comment about how they liked the book, and then place the book back on the shelf where it belongs.

3. Allow time for students to browse and discuss the books and to choose one to check out. Be available to monitor the checkout procedure and to assist with book selection as necessary.

3

Learner–Friendly Classroom Management

Classroom management not only means the organization of the physical classroom environment but also the emotional climate, atmosphere, and ambiance you wish to effectively establish. A positive climate conducive to learning will set the tone for the way students interact among themselves and with you. A positive climate evolves in part from students' sense of belonging to a classroom community and their contributions to and involvement in decision making. Their sense of ownership and belonging will impact their level of collaboration in classroom procedures. Your positive attitude, fairness, and open communication with students will affect your classroom environment.

Classroom management begins the moment students walk into the classroom the first day of school, and it evolves throughout the year. You will develop systems to effectively and efficiently organize space, schedules, and materials in order to create an orderly, cooperative, smoothly operating and well-functioning classroom.

Think again about the classroom or classrooms you worked in as a student teacher. Consider the daily and weekly management routines and procedures your cooperating teacher used and reinforced. What were the expectations of the students? How was the classroom organized? What will you do differently? What systemized routines and procedures would you like to adopt for your classroom?

WHAT IS YOUR CLASSROOM MANAGEMENT STYLE?

Your classroom management style refers to the different ways you work with students and the routines you develop to make the whole classroom environment support your teaching philosophy and instructional goals. For example, what is your level of tolerance for noise and movement in the classroom? Do you feel comfortable allowing students to talk during independent work? How much talking is too much? How much student movement around the room is appropriate? Are you more teacher centered or more learner centered? What kinds of transition activities do you have planned? How important is it for your students to move quickly, quietly, and efficiently from one activity to another? How will you handle incomplete work? How do you feel about messy desks? Calling out answers or not raising hands? Not following directions? How much independent seat work, small-group, whole-class, and cooperative group work? How teacher centered should the classroom be? How will you differentiate instruction? In what type of classroom are you personally most comfortable? Preferences such as these will influence the types and number of management expectations you outline for your students.

Your personal beliefs about student expectations for behavior, your personal teaching style, and your management style will determine the procedures and routines you feel are appropriate for students at your grade level, and they will determine how organized and structured your classroom will be. The structure and expectations of your school—and in particular, your grade level—will in part guide these decisions.

REFLECTION: WHAT IS MY PERSONAL CLASSROOM MANAGEMENT STYLE?

Visualize and describe the type of classroom in which you feel most comfortable. What does it look like? Sketch it out. What does it feel like? How do you envision students working and moving about the room?

The key to effective classroom management is to be *proactive and consistent*. Establish rules, routines, and expectations for behavior from the start. This means organizing your classroom to maximize students' engagement.

Being proactive is based on your ability to foresee instruction—to think through what organizational structures must be in place for lesson plans to go smoothly for you and the students.

Plan to be flexible. Don't be afraid to make changes when things don't work the way you wanted. On the other hand, avoid making frequent changes. Make changes only when appropriate or necessary, so students are not continually adapting to modified expectations and procedures.

Develop a resource file for classroom management ideas from conferences, books, workshops, and other teachers. You will eventually have on file several ways to carry out many routine tasks and procedures.

CLASSROOM RULES

Some teachers decide to ask students to help generate classroom rules. Getting students involved in classroom management helps make them feel responsible for what happens in the classroom. Even if you want students to share in the responsibility of deciding on classroom management routines and procedures, keep in mind that it is ultimately *your* task to make certain that the rules are adequate and appropriate. First, consider your own bottom-line expectations regarding routines and procedures before inviting students to contribute their ideas. Also, be sure to keep in mind school rules and class rules in your grade level for consistency. A number of key decisions should be made before the first day of school. Here are several essential questions to consider in establishing classroom routines and procedures:

- What initial activities will you design to have students get to know each other and begin to develop a classroom community?
- During group instruction, should students raise their hands if they want to ask or answer a question?
- Are students free to come to your desk to ask for help at any time?
- May students move around the room without permission? If so, when?
- What procedures will you establish for when students finish their work?
- How will students transition in and out of learning centers?
- How should students get help when you are busy?
- How should students enter and leave the classroom for recess, lunch, the library, PE, other specialists, and final dismissal?
- What are the homework expectations and policies of your school and grade level?
- What procedures will you put into effect for collecting and grading homework? What will you do about missing assignments?
- What should students do if they finish an assignment early?

ROUTINES

Routines allow you to operate with clear expectations and consistent procedures in a well-managed classroom. When children are confused or unsure of what to do or how to do it, the emotional climate in the classroom suffers. Routines provide needed consistency, structure, and security.

Beginning with the first day of school, decide in advance which procedures you will establish. Communicate these systems carefully to your students, so they will know what you expect, setting a specific procedure for every routine activity. Establish these procedures early, reinforce them often, and you will improve your chances of surviving your first year with energy and optimism.

It is important that children have a sense of the daily class schedule and structure. Students should know from the beginning of the school year what is routinely expected of them during the school day. Some teachers develop a schedule in which each day of the week, Monday through Friday, has its unique activities. Students soon learn this routine and know the activities for the day before even entering the room.

Begin establishing routines the first day of class. For elementary students, it is not enough to post rules on the bulletin board or even to read the rules together. Rules, routines, and procedures must be taught, demonstrated, and modeled. If the classroom management structure begins right away, it is much easier to maintain it than to attempt to establish it later in the school year. Teachers who make it clear in the first weeks of school what is expected in daily routines generally have smoother running classrooms and spend less time on organization and behavior problems throughout the year.

Students need to learn how to succeed in your classroom. Help them be successful by making it clear to them what is expected of them in typical daily situations. When may they get out of their seats? How should they get materials and supplies? When can they use the learning centers? Routines must be specific and detailed. These procedures should not only be explained but also *taught* just like any content material.

You will need to think through a routine or procedure for each of your teaching activities. Will you break up your class into smaller groups for certain subjects, such as reading, writing, or math, or do you plan small-group instruction in other subjects, too? In what sorts of hands-on, constructivist activities (e.g., science experiments and math manipulatives) will you engage students? How will you incorporate student oral reports, presentations, demonstrations, and technology presentations during the day? What lesson topics are suitable for inquiry teaching and discovery learning? Are any of your lesson ideas suitable for independent investigations or projects? Will educational games or learning centers enhance your instruction?

As an effective elementary teacher, you will vary classroom activities and pace. Teach a management procedure for each new activity to prevent confusion and to help students proceed successfully. For example, it is not enough to decide when students may use the learning centers—you must also specify details such as how many students can be in one learning center at a time, when students may change from one center to another, and what behavior is expected in learning centers (voice level, sharing, use of materials, completing projects, cleanup, etc.).

Another important routine during the school day includes how to line up quietly for recess, PE, library, assembly programs, and emergency drills. Make sure, for instance, that your students understand that they must remain in their seats until *you* dismiss them—they do not jump up to leave when the school bell rings or when the emergency signal sounds.

Daily Routines for the Start and End of the School Day

Once established, routines tend to remain the same throughout the year. Start-up routines include

- How and when students should enter the classroom;
- Where backpacks should be stored;
- What to do with homework and notes from parents;
- How attendance will be taken; and
- What students first work on.

During the day, establish procedures for

- Students arriving late to class;
- Absences and makeup-work policy;
- What to do when class work is complete;
- Putting away materials;
- Lining up;
- Dismissal;
- Getting attention ("stop, look, listen" or a "freeze and listen" signal);
- Fire and disaster drills;
- Snack, recess, and lunch; and
- Transitions to small groups or learning centers.

At the end of each school day, decide how students will be excused from their last activity of the day and your dismissal procedures. In establishing procedures and routines, be certain to take into account the school's policies and informal norms.

Interruptions

Common interruptions include student requests to use the restroom, to use the pencil sharpener, to go to the office, or to leave for a special pull-out class. Decide which procedures will work best for excusing students from your classroom and know what your school policies are for having students leave the classroom. Parents coming in and out, announcements over the loud speaker, emergency procedures, and guest visitors are other interruptions that make each day unique!

Transitions

Transitions—the times before, after, and between activities—are often the true test of your ability as a classroom manager. Many children have difficulties making transitions from one activity to the next. Unstructured "down time" can often be problematic. For some students, time not scheduled for a specific activity in a classroom is an open invitation to disruptive behavior. To effectively manage the time during transition periods, it is essential to develop clear procedures and expectations. One goal is to organize and supervise transition periods in order to maintain a smooth and brisk instructional pace that uses instructional time effectively. Your classroom management procedures should keep children engaged, alert, and busy with no time to stand or sit around with "nothing to do." Another goal is to give students notice that a change in activities is imminent to help them prepare for the transition.

The following tips can help smooth transitions:

- Be organized and ready yourself! Make sure you clearly know what the next step is in all your planning. Teachers who have the most trouble with transitions are often those who are not well organized themselves and don't have a step-by-step plan of action.
- Have a signal in place that students understand means transition time. One veteran teacher hits a small xylophone five times and then chants with the students, "Five more minutes." Her students are aware that they only have five minutes to finish up what they are involved in, and they can mentally prepare for this.
- Have all instructional materials ready, and remind your students what you expect from them as they move from one lesson to the next, such as having pencils, books, laptops, or writing journals ready. Encourage your students to clear their tables or desks of unnecessary supplies or books to prepare for the next activity.
- When giving verbal instructions to your class, be succinct and clear. Let your students know ahead of time what the plan is, so they will be ready for transitions between activities.
- Appoint monitors. These students will be the designated "materials getters" from each row or table group to help get organized during transition times. Rotate monitors regularly.
- Begin your lessons as soon as possible. Use your instructional time efficiently. Although some of your students may not be quite ready, a prompt, decisive start will encourage students to give you their full attention, and you will discourage the fooling around and time wasting that could otherwise occur. This is important for both whole-group and small-group lessons.
- Before starting a new activity, be sure most of the children have had an opportunity to complete the present one. Then, end it definitively with a summary, and bridge it to the next activity. Have activities or work planned for early finishers and those needing further challenges.
- Have clearly marked trays or other holders available for completed work. Students should know beforehand where they should place their completed work—labeled with their names and a proper heading on written work, of course. By using separate storage bins for work from each subject or project, you will feel less overwhelmed in organizing student work, checking it, and recording grades later.
- If the transition involves moving from a seated academic activity, such as reading, to a nonacademic or outside activity, such as recess, lunch, or PE, teach your students a system for how you expect them to leave the classroom.
- Ease your students into the next lesson or activity by providing a short activity. Especially after breaks such as recess or lunch, the transition is eased if students have something to do as soon as they come into the room. Place a question or activity on the whiteboard or overhead projector for students to see, so they can begin working on it immediately.

- Use sticky notes. At the end of a lesson to check for understanding and get student feedback, have students write one new thing they learned, put their name on the paper, and stick it on the whiteboard as they transition to the next activity. Have novice or reluctant writers draw a picture.

Procedures During Small-Group Instruction

Small-group instruction is intended for working with a smaller number of students who are alike in their skill development. Try to form these groups initially based on your assessments of their skills. Be flexible with your groupings of students. The groups will change frequently as students' skills develop at different paces. Your groups will be different for reading, writing, math, and other subjects. Consider the behavior issues that may arise between students working together in a group. Sometimes, your groups may not be a perfect academic match because of the need to either separate children or partner them with others. Be sensitive to children's feelings about being in certain groups. They understand who is in what group and why. Don't post their names for all to view. Keep a list for yourself to refer to. The students will soon learn which group they are in.

- Let students know when their group is to come to the teacher, instructional aide, parent, or specialist running a center. Place a schedule on the whiteboard along with each group's assignment/and or rotation. Icons and colors help younger children keep track of the schedule chart and proceed to the correct center. Try using a pocket chart to create an easily changed display of schedule cards.
- Be somewhat flexible with your timing. Although you have limited time to work with each group, some students may need more time than others to work with you to learn a new concept or finish a task. One group may be able to finish their work independently while another will need your support. If you have multiple centers working simultaneously in the classroom, do not call or signal for groups to change until you see that most of them are finished with their center's activity. If students are to bring special materials to the instructional group, let them know before they arrive.
- Before meeting with a small group, give clear instructions for work and behavior expectations to the rest of the class, including the adults that may be working with the students. If you expect children to rotate through several centers (e.g., writing, reading, math, or science), make sure you've demonstrated the specific tasks in each center. If students are choosing centers independently, set parameters for the number of participants in each center and what tasks are to be accomplished. You may wish to assign groups to centers on specific days.
- Decide on your policy toward interruptions for your groups. If students have a problem and your room is arranged in collaborative table groups, encourage students to ask each other for help. A successful policy is, "Ask three, then me." Do not respond to individual questions until the child has first asked peers, and then only *after* the small-group time is completed and you are

available to check in with students, answer questions, and monitor class work.

- Decide ahead of time—and make sure that students know—the procedure for collecting assignments completed by children not in your groups. The work might be collected by monitors or put into students' personal work folders.
- Make sure students understand what to do if assignments are finished early. Establish guidelines for what to do during these times and what free-time activities will be available. Students might sit at the listening center with headphones, read a book, work at the computer, or finish other work.

Implementing a Pattern for a Smooth Start Each Day

Start each day on a positive note. The morning routine is an important way to start each school day. A pattern or routine for beginning each day gives children a warm, comfortable welcome. Greet your children at the classroom door when they arrive in the morning, and say something personally to each child. Then, try one of the following suggestions for morning rituals:

- Conduct a daily class meeting. Sit in a semicircle in which everyone can see one another's face.
- Begin the daily calendar routines (day of the week, weather, schedule for the day).
- Sing a song together (primary grades).
- Write the morning message together, or correct one that you have already written together as a class.
- Have your students write in journals. Interactive "dialogue journals" in which you have written back to individual students are eagerly read at the start of each day.
- Schedule independent reading time.

Daily Schedule

Post a daily schedule, and review it with students each day at some point during your morning routine. This will help students know what to anticipate during the day. For many students, it is important for them to know how the day will proceed and what the schedule is. This is particularly helpful during the beginning of school for primary-age children who may tend to be more anxious about the new, and often longer, school day. Use the schedule to develop questions to help children become aware of the daily sequence of events and concepts of time, including telling time.

Questions to help your students relate the daily schedule to time could include the following:

1. What will we be doing first this morning?

2. What happens right before lunch?

3. What is the final activity for this day?

4. What time will you go to PE today?

5. What will our class be doing at 10:30?

6. What time will you go to lunch today?

You can write the daily schedule on the whiteboard. Many primary teachers make a permanent schedule display with a pocket chart (especially good if your schedule is flexible), writing time cards or clock faces and activity cards on tagboard strips. A sample daily class schedule in an elementary self-contained classroom is shown in Resource 3.1.

INCREASING YOUR EFFICIENCY WITH CLASS MONITORS

Students are an important component in maintaining classroom management and routines. Delegate as many chores to students as their age and ability will allow. Assigning students to various classroom tasks gives them a chance to assume responsibility and independence and to acquire a sense of contributing and belonging to a classroom community. It also saves you considerable time!

Depending on your management style, you may assign jobs according to the sequence of your class list or by a random lottery system. If you let children volunteer for jobs, make sure that everyone in the class participates and that everyone has some kind of job. Holding elections for class monitor positions is not recommended, as it often turns into a popularity contest; and for the children not chosen, it can be damaging to their self-esteem. All students should get a chance to contribute to the smooth operation of their classroom. Rotate students' tasks on a regular basis to allow all students the opportunity to be responsible for each task, involving all students throughout the year. For tasks requiring students to leave the room, plan on designating two students as monitors. A sample list of monitors' duties follows:

- Animal cages (keeps clean)
- Animals (feeds)
- Art (keeps supplies organized and refills materials)
- Collection (collects completed assignments)
- Computer (sets up computer program)
- Library (keeps room library in order)
- Lunch (takes lunches out to lunch table)
- Paper distribution
- Pencil sharpener (operates and empties)
- Plants (waters)
- Tape players and listening center (keeps audiotapes, accompanying books, headphones, etc., organized)

Whichever monitor positions you use, review the procedures and model the correct way of performing each task with the entire class. Consider keeping a written description of all jobs in a binder for students' reference.

TIPS FOR MOVING AHEAD WITH CLEAR COMMUNICATION

Classroom Signal

Effective teachers have a procedure to quiet their class and gain students' undivided attention. It is often called a "freeze and listen" signal. For example, you might flick the lights, ring a bell, or clap your hands. The students freeze (stop whatever they're doing), turn, and look at you. Demonstrate and practice your chosen procedure until all your students understand the "stop, look, and listen" expectations.

You might create a classroom signal to call the class to order that all the students *imitate*. Many teachers use a simple gesture such as a raised hand with "peace sign" fingers or a series of rhythmic claps. One successful teacher instructs her children, "Put your finger on your nose when you hear me." When she needs their attention, she places the tip of her index finger on the tip of her nose, and her students follow suit. Another teacher uses the gentle sound of a rain stick to quiet the class. Another teacher beats a Congo drum rhythmically until all the children have joined her in clapping to the rhythm. Whatever signal you use, be consistent, and praise the class for their responsiveness to the signal.

Giving Directions

- Be clear and concise when giving students directions. Expect students to listen and follow directions the first time you have given them. Some students, however, will need you to repeat directions, and some students with limited English will need you to demonstrate what you expect while you give verbal directions.
- Many parents complain that their children do not respond to their directions at home, and these parents complain that they have to repeat themselves over and over. Do not give in to this! Expect your students to listen and follow directions immediately.
  - o Give students some kind of warning that the current activity is ending and that they will need to refocus their attention on you.
  - o Limit yourself, when possible, to only two directions at a time for any given activity. This will help your students listen and implement the activity more effectively. For example, you might say, "Please clear your desks. Then, take out your snacks."
- Get the attention of every student (as much as you can) before giving directions.
- Use both oral and written directions. Some children process information more visually and need to see directions written. Other children are more auditory learners and need to hear your clearly spoken directions.
- After giving directions, check for understanding. Ask students to repeat back what they understood your directions were.

Before students proceed with independent activities, be sure they know

- Where to get necessary materials;
- What to do if they have a question;

- Where to work;
- Where to put finished work; and
- What to do when they are finished.

KEEP YOUR CLASSROOM RUNNING SMOOTHLY WHILE YOU ARE BUSY

Sometimes during the school day, you may be forced to divert your attention away from your class instruction to something else pressing without prior notice. During a typical day in any classroom, many moments are lost while waiting in line for the bell to ring, changing from one subject to another, waiting to go to recess or home at the end of the day, and so on. These extra minutes can be used for quick review and practice activities called "sponges." To help students focus their attention while you are occupied, have ready one or two short, interesting activities listed on the whiteboard or overhead projector. Often oral, sometimes written, the objective here is to keep the students occupied as you squeeze in a bit of learning. See Resource 3.2 for some of these sponge activities.

Tips for Making Your Classroom Learner-Friendly

- Be sure that you can see all the students and that they can each see and hear you.
- Keep frequently used materials and student supplies readily accessible: pencil sharpener, trash cans, recycling bins, frequently used supplies (e.g., paper, pencils, markers, crayons, scissors, glue sticks).
- Be sure that all students can see instructional displays and presentations.
- Provide a designated area for students' personal belongings (hats, coats, lunches, etc.).

SETTING EXPECTATIONS

Your Goals for the First Days of School

As you look forward to the first days of school, set goals regarding classroom management. Your success during the entire school year is often determined by what you do during the opening days of school. The first two or three weeks of school are critical in determining how well students will behave and achieve during the remainder of the year! It is essential to set high expectations for your students and establish firm classroom procedures and understandable routines during these first few weeks. Keep in mind that your teaching accountability goes beyond content matter. Developing responsible students who demonstrate positive behavior is also a critical part of your job.

Important goals during the first days of school include:

1. Getting to know your students;
2. Students' getting to know you and each other; and
3. Classroom organization and management.

Getting to Know Your Students

- Maintain a whole-group focus in instruction.
- Actively engage all students in learning activities.
- Begin assessing students to better understand their academic abilities.
- Take time to get to know students in small groups and individually.

Students' Getting to Know You and Each Other

- Establish an accepting classroom climate; demonstrate respect, caring, and personal interest.
- Design lessons to ensure that all students feel successful. Keep activities simple but significant. Hands-on activities resulting in a product or a sense of productivity are especially beneficial.
- Plan activities to help students introduce themselves to each other. See Resources 3.3, 3.4, 3.5, and 3.6 for good start-of-year activities. Use other interest inventories, multiple intelligence inventories, partner interviews, personal perspective presentations, All About Me posters or slide shows, and learning inventories to learn more about students and to provide fun ways for students to learn about each other.

Classroom Organization and Management

- Direct your attention to establishing routines and procedures.
- Teach appropriate behavior, rules, procedures, consequences, and attention signals. Practice each routine.
- Acquaint students with the room and materials they will use (supplies, books, etc.).
- Explain policies regarding homework, missed assignments, and absences.
- Preview curriculum highlights as a motivational device. Do something fun within the first month!

ON THE OPENING DAY

- Dress professionally but comfortably.
- Pack some healthy snacks for recess or break time and a big lunch!
- Be at school at least one hour early.
- Make sure your name is posted outside your classroom door.
- Spend time with anxious parents (especially at the primary level) who accompany children to school.
- Stand by the door to greet each student with a welcoming smile.
- Know how to pronounce and spell correctly the name of each student in your class, and check for nicknames parents and students use regularly.
- Label cubbies, desks, books, and other materials students will need. Note: Some teachers wait until the end of the first day to label things in the event students do not show up to school, students have name changes due to nicknames, you get last-minute new students, or you decide to change seating or cubby arrangements once you meet your students.
- Place a fun, easy-to-do activity sheet on each desk for students to complete while you greet latecomers and say good-bye to parents at the door.

RESOURCE 3.1

Sample Daily Class Schedule

	Monday	*Tuesday*	*Wednesday*	*Thursday*	*Friday*
8:15–8:45	Opening (community circle), attendance, classroom duties				
8:45–10:30	Reading/language arts Journal writing/writer's workshop Spelling/"word work"				
10:30–10:45	Recess and snack				
10:45–11:00	Read aloud to class				
11:00–12:00	Math				
12:00–12:45	Lunch and recess				
12:45–1:15	Independent work, reading conferences with teacher, peer tutoring/conferences				
1:15–2:15	Writing (prewriting and draft)	Science/social studies	Writing (finish drafting and authors' circle)	Science/social studies	Writing (revise, edit, share)
2:15–3:15	PE	Science/social studies	PE	Science/social studies	Art
3:15–3:30	Author's chair, announcements, cleanup, dismissal				

RESOURCE 3.2

Sponge Activities

- List as many states as you can.
- List as many countries and their capitals as you can.
- Write down as many cartoon characters as you can.
- Draw and label as many kinds of flowers as you can.
- List all the things in your living room.
- List as many nouns in this room as you can.
- Draw and label five things you do after school.
- List one proper noun for each letter of the alphabet.
- List as many U.S. presidents as you can.
- Draw and label as many kinds of trees as you can.
- Name and draw as many breeds of dogs as you can.
- Correct your homework (answers can be placed on the board or an overhead).
- Ask, "What comes between these two numbers?" For example, 31 and 33, 45 and 47, and so forth.
- Ask, "What number comes before/after 46 (53, 32, etc.)?"
- Ask, "What month of the year has the most syllables? What city in our state, which student's name in our class, and which teacher's name in our school has the most syllables in its name?"
- Write a word on the board and have students make a list of words that rhyme with it.
- Have students put spelling words in alphabetical order.
- Have students count to 100 (or as far as they can) by twos, fives, tens—either orally with a buddy or in writing.
- Have students say the sevens table in multiplication. Then eights. Then nines.
- Have students think of animals that live on a farm, in the jungle, in the water, and so forth.
- Write a word on the board. Have children list words with the same long or short vowel sound.
- Have students scramble five spelling or vocabulary words, trade with someone, and unscramble the words.
- Tell students, "Write a dialogue between _____ and _____."

RESOURCE 3.3

Start-of-Year Activities

ACTIVITIES FOR STARTING THE YEAR

Inheritance Fantasy

This activity gives you a writing sample and often reveals interesting facets of a student's personality.

Have students write a paragraph telling what they would do if they won $10,000 with the restriction that they could keep only half and must give the other half away. They need to explain who would get the other half and why.

Guess Who I Am

This is a great "getting to know you" activity for the first week.

Have each student write autobiographical information on an index card and give them to you. You write one out, too. Then, read one card aloud each day and have the students guess who the person is.

Forced Choice

This is a fun activity for any age group. It works anytime during the year but is especially worthwhile during the first few days. Students feel comfortable doing this activity and get to know each other in the process. The activity can be written or done orally with younger children.

Students are given two choices (see suggestions below). They must choose one and give a reason for doing so. One effective way to do this activity is to physically use the space in your classroom. After giving the two options, ask the children to go to the side of the room identified for that option. There, they can talk to other students who share their choice. (In the upper grades, the kids could start by writing out their reasons and then grouping together by choice afterward.) Following are some suggestions for choice options:

Are you a/an:	kite string	or	clothesline?
	addition sign	or	multiplication sign?
	Goofy	or	Mickey?
	ALF	or	Batman?
	president	or	captain?
	Hershey's Kiss	or	Snickers?
	skateboard	or	roller skates?
	Reebok	or	Nike?
	rock-n-roller	or	rapper?
	banana split	or	milkshake?
	roller coaster	or	Ferris wheel?

RESOURCE 3.4

Start-of-Year Activities: All About Me

ALL ABOUT ME

Write your answers now in the first column. Then, we will do it again in the spring in the second column. Fold your paper down the middle.

1. Date _____	_____
2. Full name _____	_____
3. Favorite kind of pizza _____	_____
4. My favorite color _____	_____
5. My favorite place _____	_____
6. My favorite singer _____	_____
7. My favorite sport to play _____	_____
8. I like to _____	_____
9. My favorite game _____	_____
10. My favorite TV show _____	_____
11. When I grow up, I'll _____	_____
12. I like to spend time _____	_____
13. My favorite animal _____	_____
14. My favorite celebrity _____	_____

RESOURCE 3.5

Start-of-Year Activities: People Hunt

PEOPLE HUNT

Hunt for someone who can say yes to one of these questions. Have this person sign his or her name. Can you find a different person for each line?

1. Can whistle _____
2. Has an older brother _____
3. Can run a six-minute mile _____
4. Is wearing blue _____
5. Loves to cook _____
6. Is new to our school this year _____
7. Enjoys reading _____
8. Plays guitar _____
9. Lost a tooth this summer _____
10. Played baseball this summer _____
11. Made a sand castle this summer _____
12. Has ridden on a train _____
13. Had a birthday in July _____
14. Has a birthday in October _____
15. Speaks three languages _____
16. Recycles at home _____
17. Wears reading glasses _____
18. Has a pet cat _____
19. Has an aquarium _____
20. Loves yogurt _____
21. Is left handed _____
22. Wants to be a scientist _____
23. Likes to swim _____
24. Wants to be an orthodontist _____
25. Has a turkey sandwich packed for lunch _____
26. Has visited New York _____
27. Likes to play soccer _____
28. Has a great-grandfather _____
29. Plays the piano _____
30. Likes to sing _____

RESOURCE 3.6

Start-of-Year Activities: Interest Inventory

INTEREST INVENTORY

Name: _____ Grade: _____ Date: _____

1. What activities do you most like to do at home?

   _____

   _____

2. If your parents told you that you could do anything you wanted to do this weekend, what would you choose?

   _____

   _____

3. What do you think you are really good at outside of school?

   _____

   _____

4. What do you think you are really good at in school?

   _____

   _____

5. What do you think is really hard for you outside of school?

   _____

   _____

6. What subject is most difficult for you in school?

   _____

   _____

7. If you could learn about anything you wanted to learn about, what would you choose?

   _____

   _____

8. If you could change three things at school, what would they be?

   _____

   _____

9. What is your favorite thing to do with your friends outside of school?

_____

_____

10. What book have you read recently that was really exciting for you?

_____

_____

11. What is your favorite sport to play?

_____

_____

12. Do you like to do your homework alone, with a partner, or in a small group?

_____

_____

13. What time do you go to bed during the week?

_____

_____

14. What would you like to be and do when you grow up?

_____

_____

15. If you were granted three wishes, what would you wish for?

_____

_____

4

Behavior Management and Discipline

Managing and Monitoring Student Behavior

Discipline is an integral part of teaching. It is also the most frequently reported concern of beginning teachers. It typically has an ominous connotation. You know intuitively that without the confidence and skill to discipline students you will not be able to teach successfully. Effective discipline and effective instruction are inseparable. It is often said that *one can't teach until one deals with behavior.* New teachers frequently share this sentiment, reporting that they spend too much of their time dealing with student behavior, leaving little time for actual teaching. However, discipline and instruction need not be dichotomous, and discipline does not have to be punitive. It can be a positive and productive aspect of teaching. Establishing classroom conditions to which students respond with respect and cooperation is as much a part of discipline as authoritarian monitoring, controlling, and intervening.

You have undoubtedly started your teaching career with vows to be good humored, fair minded, and enthusiastic. You plan learning activities that will energize students' positive behavior and intrinsic motivation. You will accommodate variety and individual differences and make your lessons relevant to students' lives. You will use time effectively, choosing academic tasks conducive to high student engagement. You will implement grouping strategies for high levels of involvement and low levels of misbehavior. You will communicate rules of participation clearly. Your classroom climate, planning, and instruction will have a major effect in preventing discipline problems.

Discipline is much more than spotting and punishing misbehavior. Your primary behavior management task is to establish and maintain positive classroom practices. Rules, procedures, routines, and consequences all have a role to play, but they can only supplement what you do to orchestrate your overall instructional program.

How you manage and monitor student behavior is closely linked to your teaching philosophy. Reflect on the behaviors and attributes you want to promote among your students (e.g., respect, responsibility, and collaboration), and develop a discipline plan that supports your ideals. Become familiar with different approaches to discipline that work for you and your students.

More than a dozen discipline models of varying degrees of structure have been developed. They range along a continuum from those that are predominantly student centered and use psychotherapeutic and communication principles to those that are decidedly teacher centered and are based on behavioral psychology. Read recommended books and articles on discipline techniques and programs. Discuss what works to promote desirable behavior, and share concerns and problems with colleagues. Effective behavior management begins with an attitude that you can and will do something about inappropriate behavior. Being proactive and not reactive puts you in charge—insisting on but also assisting in creating order in a calm, professional manner.

School Discipline Policies

Know what you can and cannot do. Consider district and school policies on student discipline when establishing your class rules.

Observe the informal norms of your school, and discuss these with your mentor or principal. Ask your school administrator for a copy of the teacher handbook, parent handbook, and/or student handbook for your district's approved model, such as "assertive discipline." Some schools operate as structured, controlled, rather authoritarian systems; others are more relaxed, enfranchised, and even permissive. Ask about the school-wide discipline plan. How consistent is it? Do teachers enforce the established school rules? Does the principal want to get involved in discipline referrals? Is a time-out or detention room used? Is it effective? Get to know your school's and community's prevailing culture concerning discipline expectations. You will be expected to follow the district system. As a new teacher, you will have to learn not to take negative behavior personally. A student's choice to break a rule is not usually an expression of dislike or a reflection of your ability or personality. Once you realize this, behavior management becomes easier.

Teaching Standards of Behavior and Establishing Rules

The way in which students act is their behavior; the principles that govern expected actions are rules. Before creating classroom rules, think deeply about the standards of behavior you want to establish and expect from students. Create the classroom environment you feel best meets students' learning needs. In doing so, you integrate your beliefs about conditions that help students learn (academic, behavioral, social, and emotional) within the practical limitations of the setting.

Typical standards of behaviors include using a quiet voice, responding to a signal, knowing how to line up, and knowing what to do when the teacher is busy. Start by brainstorming a list of behaviors you want to see in your classroom. Then, select the most appropriate for your specific class. You will probably need to establish priorities, however. Cut the list down to the five or six most important behaviors. You may have 10 to 15 you will eventually want to teach, but save some for later. What do you want first? Clearly define, model, and have students practice desired behaviors. Be sure to positively praise students every time they execute the correct standard of behavior. Teaching desirable behavior, just as you teach any lesson, is an excellent way to promote it. For example, a norm that most teachers have in their classrooms is "responding to a signal." As you do with content, you need to first define this learning. What exactly does *respond to the signal* mean? The process for teaching it may look like this:

1. Make sure students know the signal (saying, "May I have your attention please?" or ringing a bell, flicking the lights, holding an arm high, etc.). Explain the signal. Model it. Have students describe and model it.

2. Make sure students know what to do (pause, stop whatever they are doing, quiet down, and look at the teacher). Discuss the procedure with the students. Choose a student to model it. Have all the students demonstrate it. Have them visualize what the class will look like after the signal is given.

3. Make sure students know when to respond. List sample class activities. Get students into an activity, and then give the signal. Have the whole group practice responding to the signal.

The key to teaching a behavior is specifying the subskills needed to complete it properly. Occasionally, an exasperated teacher will declare, "You know how you're supposed to behave!" Unfortunately, this is not always true. You must clearly define the behavior and what is expected of students. Nobody should have to guess. Establishing rules goes hand in hand with teaching expected behaviors. Rules must make sense to you and your students. Many teachers find it desirable to have their students participate in the brainstorming of classroom rules—this gives children a sense of ownership. Students who have some control over establishing rules tend to follow the rules more often. In most cases, students arrive at the same set of rules you originally planned. Be sure to state rules in *positive and observable* terms—what students *will* do in their class. For instance, say, "Resolve disagreements by talking," rather than, "No fighting." Limit children to about five rules. Avoid the impression that you are more interested in defining restrictions than in promoting learning.

Once you, and your class, decide what the rules and responsibilities will be, spend time during the first weeks of school setting specific expectations. Teach the rules, consequences, and procedures; practice and model correct behaviors; and distinctly discuss unacceptable behaviors (without pointing out specific students). Remember that telling is not teaching; students often do not remember by simply being told what to do. Students need to understand clearly what behavior is expected. They need to discuss the behavior and see it demonstrated. Some examples of common rules (with discussion points) are shown below.

- *Speak to fellow classmates with respect.* Discussion points: People's feelings are not for hurting. Put-downs in this room are forbidden. Teasing others is not OK.
- *Keep your hands and feet to yourself.* Discussion points: It is inappropriate to touch classmates, including pushing, shoving, wrestling, and tripping. No throwing of objects—pencils, erasers, rubber bands—at another person, either! Resolve any disagreements by *talking.*
- *Take care of your desk, classroom, and learning materials.* Discussion points: Keep your desk clean and organized. Put materials where they belong. Know where your books, paper, and pencils are. Respect the property of others.
- *Raise your hand for permission to speak.* Discussion points: Raise your hand and wait until you are called on to speak. This rule will not be in effect, however, during small-group discussions, class meetings, and so forth.
- *Stay in your seat unless you have permission to leave it.* Discussion points: When does the teacher say it is OK to move around the classroom? Report directly to the assigned area or center. Change from one area to the next quickly and quietly.
- *Listen the first time instructions are given.* Discussion points: Wait for directions with no talking. Be quiet whenever someone else is speaking. Eyes on the teacher whenever the teacher is giving directions.

Effective teachers discuss with their students why rules are needed, provide reasonable explanations for each rule, and explain how the rules will help everyone succeed by making the class run smoothly. Post (in large print) the basic classroom rules. Let everyone sign the rules poster. Give each student a copy. Post a copy to your class website if you have one. Send a letter or e-mail attachment to parents explaining your classroom rules. Then, ensure that the rules are followed firmly, fairly, and consistently. Be sure to revisit and review the rules periodically throughout the year.

Regular reinforcement of the rules is definitely needed. As often as possible, try to "catch the students being good," a phrase commonly used for the reinforcement of appropriate behaviors. If students are already raising hands in a discussion, you might say, "You're all doing a great job of raising hands. That allows me to call on individuals, and everybody gets a chance to think." Positive reinforcement increases the probability of that behavior recurring. When students "forget" the rules, they probably have not been positively reinforced for following them. One veteran teacher keeps a reinforcement sheet on her desk and records the number of times she has caught each student being good. It also reminds her how many times she has reviewed the rules. Rule review is often necessary at high-excitement times, such as right before or after holidays and before school ends.

In addition to carefully thinking through your classroom rules, discussing them with your students, and teaching and modeling them, you also need to consider *consequences*. What will happen if students break a rule? Consequences for unacceptable behavior should be logical and appropriate. They should fit the behavior in a sensible way. For instance, children who are running in the classroom or hallway must turn around and retrace their steps by *walking* the same route. Children who continue to thump their neighbors with a pencil are removed to seats away from the table group (and thus are unable to contribute "table points" and participate in the day's group reward). Students who write on the desk must stay in at recess and clean the desk. For consequences to be effective, students must see them as logically and naturally related to their misbehavior. A time-out is often a logical consequence. A place out of sight (but not out of sight of the teacher) reduces the emotional impact of the situation, does not lead to escalation, and allows the student a chance to calm down.

When logical consequences are invoked, your voice is friendly and implies good will. Rather than communicating typical negative messages of punishment ("You're bad," "You'll never learn," "You're not acceptable," "You deserve what you're getting," "You'd better shape up," "I'll show you!" etc.), treat the student with dignity, separate the deed from the doer, and communicate respect ("I don't like what you're doing right now, but I still trust you," "You are a worthwhile person," "I'm sure you will learn to respect the rights of others," "I trust you to make responsible choices," etc.). The purpose of using natural and logical consequences is to motivate children to make responsible decisions; it is not to force their submission. Consequences will be effective if you avoid having hidden motives of winning and controlling.

Tips for Establishing Consequences

- Explain consequences ahead of time.
- Be clear and specific.
- Have a range of proportional alternatives to make the penalty fit the infraction.
- Consequences should not be arbitrary or viewed as punishment.
- Consequences should not be related to lowering of academic grades.
- Consequences should be related directly and immediately to a rule.
- Consequences should follow naturally and logically from the misbehavior.

Students must believe that you will enforce rules consistently and administer the appropriate consequence. Your goal is to be fair, but that might mean not applying *identical* consequences. If students frequently fail to return homework, you may apply a different consequence than you would to students who forgot their homework for the first time. It is possible to be fair but not rigidly *equal*. Students can understand that *fair* and *equal* are not always the same. To be consistently fair, however, be certain that the consequences you apply are reasonable and appropriate.

Using Preventive Discipline

Behavior management is more than reacting to problems. It is the total organization of the classroom and the way you communicate that organization to students to promote desirable behavior. What you do to *prevent* negative behavior, rather than *how* you punish, makes you an effective teacher.

Students' behavior during the first week or two of school is usually good. Use this time to your advantage. Begin the year by establishing positive routines and activities to keep students motivated and avoid problems.

- Start fresh every day. What happened yesterday is finished. Act accordingly.
- Reward appropriate behavior.
- Create a warm, friendly atmosphere. Firmness does not negate a warm, personalized classroom.
- Schedule a quiet activity between recess and independent seatwork.
- Alternate between passive and active activities.
- If a planned activity is out of the normal range of expectations (such as a field trip or lab experiment), take plenty of time before the activity begins to establish behavior responsibilities.
- Establish the signal that calls the whole class to immediate attention. Practice using this signal until you get the expected "freeze and listen" behavior. Some teachers allow the students to choose the word or signal. It may be changed to reflect seasons, holidays, or units of study.
- Communicate to students that you know what is going on. This is called "with-it-ness." It is like having "eyes in the back of your head."
- Develop your ability to deal with more than one thing at a time. For example, if you are working with an individual or small group, and you spot inappropriate behavior somewhere else in the class, keep the individuals focused on the task while at the same time dealing with the disruption.
- Maintain a consistent flow in lessons. Effective teachers tend to ignore minor distractions and stay on target. They keep the lesson activities going in a smooth, consistent manner. Momentum can be lost, for instance, when a lesson is stopped to attend to a behavior problem. Frequently the rest of the students become restless as they wait for the lesson to resume.
- Avoid putting yourself in a power struggle with students. A quiet, private conference later is always preferable to confronting students in front of their peers. Similarly, avoid making threats that you cannot carry out or imposing arbitrary consequences.
- Modify your instruction to match students' abilities. Many students react negatively to work that appears too difficult, too easy, or pointless.
- Maintain student interest in lesson activities. Interest increases attention to the task. When lessons vary, when they are interesting, when the environment is changed, when you use different techniques for overt responses, when you group and regroup students, and when you do things differently in the mode of presentation, students are more likely to be engaged and involved and are less likely to cause discipline problems.

- By all means, listen to what students are saying. Students misbehave not only when they are bored but also when they feel angry or fearful. Discuss problems to help students understand and solve them. You need to find out what the problem is, so you can deal with it more effectively.
- Develop individual plans for students for whom your classwide system does not work (e.g., learning or behavior contracts—addressed later in the chapter).

Praise

One of the easiest and most underutilized proactive behavior management strategies is the use of teacher praise. Used properly, teacher praise can effectively increase desirable student behavior. Your objective in using praise is to help children develop an internal locus of control to improve behavior and academic effort and achievement. Praise should be focused on behavior and efforts and not solely on outcomes and achievement. Praise also should be frequent, immediate, and specific, describing for the student the exact nature of the behavior being rewarded. Suggested uses of praise include the following:

- Give praise for desired behavior and define the behavior: "Thank you for picking up the papers. You really helped the class save time."
- Specify what is praiseworthy about the student's schoolwork. Always give a reason when praising a student's learning performance: "You blended the blues and greens in the sky beautifully—it really shows your knowledge of color groups." "Kevin read that paragraph so expressively that I could almost feel the pain myself."
- Praise effort over outcomes. All students, regardless of academic achievement levels, can increase their level of effort. Praising students' efforts will serve to build intrinsic motivation.
- Vary your praise and be creative. Avoid trite, general words, such as *great, fine,* and *wonderful.* Also ineffective are the too lavish, too strong, and gushy tones.
- At times, give praise privately to avoid competition, embarrassment, or singling someone out as teacher's pet. Many teachers of intermediate students have more success delivering quiet individual praise rather than praising individuals before the whole class.
- Praise needs to be genuine and matched by your body language. Be consistent with your verbal and nonverbal praise. The teacher who says a student is doing a terrific job but reflects insincere body language has "erased" the verbal praise. Remember, body language accounts for 70% of the message.
- Teach students to authentically praise one another's efforts. Take time at the end of a project for students to share positive comments and praise: "John really made sure that his illustrations matched his writing."
- Stop halfway through a project and have students take a "gallery-walk" around the classroom looking at each other's work in progress. Have students share comments about other's progress. It is equally important that praise comes during an effort in addition to upon completion of an effort.

- Avoid teacher-pleasing phrases, such as "I really like the way you used descriptive words in your poem." A more powerful message is, "You did an excellent job of using descriptive words in your story. The reader can really hear and see what you meant." Many teachers use too many *I* statements when praising, such as, "I like the way you're listening (working, raising hands, lining up, writing, etc.)." Instead, say, "You're listening so well; you'll do it just right!"
- Do not use sarcastic and insincere praise.
- Do not minimize a child's success. Watch out for statements such as, "Your math assignment must have been easy. You finished so quickly."

Dealing With Misbehavior

No matter how meticulously you have planned and taught behavioral standards and class rules, you will likely have to deal with inappropriate student behavior eventually. As an effective classroom manager, you must handle misbehavior immediately and smoothly to prevent a snowballing effect—instead of one or two students being involved, soon there may be several. Students will test the rules to find out whether you will enforce them. Follow through, and mean what you say. Children will quickly violate a rule they see classmates violating unless you step in. To provide maximum time for learning and reduce minor behavior problems, here are some strategies to employ that deal with misbehavior in the least amount of time, with the least disruption, and with the least negative feelings arising.

- Look at the offending student directly with prolonged eye contact while you continue your lesson.
- Shake your head to stress your message to the student.
- Stop talking for a few seconds.
- Use proximity. Continue your lesson as you move about the room, pausing near "trouble spots."
- Try not to make a big deal out of it. "Soft reprimands," not causing a major commotion while you deliver your feelings of displeasure to a student, will often successfully suppress the misbehavior and also save the student's self-concept.
- Be aware of your options, such as the following:
  o Are time-outs in the hall allowed in your school?
  o Can you send students to the office for detention or keep students in during recess or after school? In what cases should the principal be involved in your discipline procedures?

- Consider changing students' seats or schedule if problems persist.
- Take away privileges, not educational experiences. It might take only these words: "You may choose a free-time activity when you finish your work."

In general, when dealing with serious misbehavior, you should talk less and act *more*. Many beginning teachers hinder their effectiveness in discipline by talking too much. Students easily become "teacher deaf" from the continuous sound of the teacher's voice. Do most of your talking with students when you are on friendly terms and they are therefore more willing to listen. When dealing with misbehavior and using logical consequences, keep talk to a minimum as you follow through with action.

Be both firm and kind. Your tone of voice indicates your desire to be kind while your follow-through with appropriate action indicates your firmness. Remain as matter of fact as you can. If you can view misbehavior objectively, rather than regarding it as a personal affront, you will be more effective.

MOTIVATING YOUR STUDENTS

Motivation is often described as the desire to seek and conquer challenges. Sources for motivation can be characterized as intrinsic or extrinsic. While external motivators, such as earning points, rewards, and/or tokens, can and does motivate some students to comply with behavioral expectations, these systems can be complex, time intensive, and are dependent on the absolute consistency of implementation to be effective. For the majority of learners, extrinsic motivators are not necessary for increasing student interest and motivation to learn. Many veteran teachers recognize the importance of building students' intrinsic motivation—the desire to choose and complete an activity just for the sake and satisfaction of the activity itself. As you begin your career in education, strive to create a classroom environment that fosters students to be intrinsically motivated.

- Begin with your classroom's physical environment. Is it a student-centered work environment that supports collaboration and peer interaction? Have you arranged learning centers, students' desks, tables, and furniture to support interaction? Do you regularly introduce different books and new materials in your learning centers? Do the walls show interesting displays, current student work, and interactive learning tools such as word walls, a calendar, and morning messages? In short, is your classroom a place to which students want to come and actively learn?
- Consider the feeling tone of the classroom—how pleasant does the learning environment and the particular learning situations feel to the students? A safe, accepting environment enables all children to feel free to take risks, learn, and grow.
- Do you involve students in decisions that affect their lives at school? Regularly giving students choices is a great way to increase personal motivation. The choices offered to students need not be different than the choices that could have been selected by the teacher. Allow students to choose a book for *read aloud* from a selection of five to six different titles. Give a group of students a choice of two or three different math games at a learning center. During independent seatwork, offer students a choice from a small menu of activities. This can be as simple as letting students choose from a selection of worksheets. As you can see, the choices you offer students do not need to alter the direction of your learning objectives. As you write your lesson plans, look for simple places where you could embed student choice. No matter

how small or insignificant these choices seem on the surface, they will go a great way toward building intrinsic motivation.

- Capitalize on students' interests. When teaching a lesson on cursive writing, practice words and sentences of topics favored by students. Note the kinds of books your students select from the library, and keep those genres and titles in your classroom for independent reading. Focus writing lessons on teaching genre and structure, and leave the topic selection up to the individual student.

- Do you encourage your students to participate in a range of classroom activities and projects? Do you teach for all the multiple intelligences and learning modalities? Are students regularly given opportunities to use higher-order thinking skills (e.g., create, compare, assemble)?

- Have you displayed student work throughout your room? Do you (and/or the students) change it regularly? Are students pleased with what they accomplish in your room? Do they feel successful? Do you emphasize what each child knows and contributes?

- If some of your students complete work earlier than their classmates, do you resist the temptation to hand them worksheets to keep them occupied? Are you conscientious about providing meaningful learning alternatives, such as time on the computer, working quietly at a learning center or the art center, sitting in the class library corner for free reading, and so on? Try asking the students how they would like to use this time. Teach students how to make good use of their extra time, and empower them by trusting their choices.

- Do you help students develop pride in themselves, the class, and the room? Do you praise their efforts in completing difficult tasks and invite parents and/or another class to see your students' new play, science experiment, writing display, or art exhibit?

- Do you send e-mails home sharing some specific and positive praise about a student? Communication with parents often focuses on misbehavior. Try sending a "Your Child Was Caught Doing Something Good" e-mail.

- Do you remember to smile, give a high five, a pat, a handshake, or a word of encouragement? Listen reflectively and genuinely? Give compliments and ask questions relating to children's personal interests and experiences? Let them know you care?

How you attempt to motivate your students depends on your educational philosophy, and it relates to that mental image of how you want your classroom to feel. Student motivation stems from an enjoyable, interesting class with a positive, personable, genuinely caring teacher.

Instructional Variety Is Important

A variety of learning activities keeps students interested in school and their schoolwork. Student interest is a powerful motivator. Students who are interested in what they are doing will enjoy it more, do it longer, and learn more from it. When students are interested and engaged in learning activities, they feel more successful, and you have less worry about behavior management and discipline.

A good way to increase student motivation is to vary your instructional methods. As a new teacher, you are probably aware of some teachers' overuse of one instructional method, often a sequence of lectures, convergent questions, and individual seat work. Such teachers seem to forget that students have different learning styles, attitudes, interests, and backgrounds. Do not slip into the habit of relying on only one or two tried-and-true favorite methods. As you plan a lesson or a unit, look for ways to add variety.

You might begin by reviewing the list of sample strategies and resources below. Is it possible to incorporate one or more into a unit, for example? This list may spark your creative thinking.

Advertisement	ePal correspondence	Newsletter
Artifact	Experiment	Pantomime
Autobiography	Fantasy	Pets
Bingo	Field research	Play
Book review	Flip book	Podcast
Case study	Flow chart	Puppets
Choral reading	Game show	Quiz
Comedy	iMovie	Reader's Theater
Competition	Invention	Replica
Computers	Jigsaw	Simulation
Crafts	Letter to expert	Survey
Debate	Lyric or Rap	Video
Demonstration	Modeling	Webpage
Diagram	Montage	Webquest
Dialogue	Myth	

Questions to Consider for Improving Motivation

- Is competition a good way to motivate individuals or groups?
- Is teamwork a good way to motivate individuals or groups?
- How does self-esteem relate to student motivation?
- How does the relevancy of the lesson—for students—relate to student motivation?
- How does the execution of the lesson relate to student motivation?
- When might external rewards be used? With whom?

MANAGING STUDENT BEHAVIOR

Conflict Resolution

Negative interactions between and among students can be quite common yet effectively circumvented with explicit and frequent instruction in conflict resolution. Conflicts, especially between younger students, are frequently the result of not having developed interpersonal skills. For many kindergarten students, school may be their first experience having to share materials, waiting for turn taking, or even following what may feel like too many rules. Feelings are easily hurt, and conflicts result. As students mature and social relationships become more complex, frequent instruction in conflict resolution continues to be a vital aspect of your behavior management program.

Instruction in conflict resolution includes lots of teacher modeling followed by ample opportunities for students to role-play how to handle themselves in specific situations. Scenarios are fictitious but resemble actual student problems occuring in the grade you teach. Essentially, your job is to become a facilitator as students actively learn to take responsibility for and solve conflicts independently. With consistent practice, students will begin to internalize the way in which they can resolve conflict independently and peacefully.

Setting the Scene for Instruction

Lessons in conflict resolution should never occur during an actual incident. Tempers may be flared, and students may not be in a proactive-learning frame of mind. Schedule conflict resolution lessons just as you would schedule any other weekly lesson or as a result of a recent incident that provides a good opportunity for learning. Another critical aspect of conflict resolution training is to keep it from becoming personal. If students detect that you may be referring to a previous classroom incident in which they were involved, they may feel embarrassed and defensive. Using literature to provide the context of the lesson is a very effective strategy. Teaching conflict resolution through literature allows students to analyze the problem, identify and evaluate specific behaviors used by the characters, and develop alternative solutions. You may even use the literature-based scenarios as a springboard for role-playing. Students can reenact the conflict using the same or more effective behaviors as the characters in the text. A wide range of literature targeting specific age levels and sources of conflict is readily available in your library and local bookstore. Refer to Resource 4.1 for a list of titles. Many teachers label a basket or a special section of a bookshelf to keep these texts accessible for weekly lessons.

Changing Inappropriate Behavior of Individual Students

To deal with individual disruptive behavior—the student who consistently insists on making the wrong choices—you need to implement a strategy. Here is a specific plan you can use to change student behavior.

1. Identify the Problem and Collect Objective Data

Suppose your class has the rule "Remain in line and walk quietly to recess," but Shawn keeps running out the door, pushing kids, cutting to the front, and so on. Start by noting the frequency to make the problem clear to the student and, sometimes, the parent. Using an index card to make tally marks is a quick method.

2. Select an Appropriate Consequence and Positive Reinforcer

The question to ask yourself is, "What doesn't Shawn want?" Simply charting the behavior can sometimes be an appropriate consequence. The student sees the result of your watchful eye immediately. Staying in at recess may be an appropriate consequence. A positive reinforcement may be a coveted task, such as being line leader or calendar person for a day. A note or call home may also be necessary.

3. Conduct a Conference With the Student (and/or Principal, Other Teachers, and Parents)

This is the most important part of the process. The student must hear the problem, see the frequency, know the consequences, and explain or demonstrate the appropriate behavior ("What does *remain in line and walk quietly to recess* mean, Shawn? Tell me what you'll do in line," etc.).

4. Set Up Successful Situations to "Catch the Student Being Good"

Be consistent with reinforcement strategies. When Shawn comes in the next day, remind him quietly, "What are you going to do, Shawn? I'm going to keep track of how well you remember." Sometimes, the student can keep a personal chart on successfully making or not making the appropriate choice.

5. Reinforce Regularly

Reinforce positively with social rewards (praise, smiles, an approving nod) every time a student remembers at first. Later, move to intermittent reinforcement. When will Shawn forget? Probably near holidays and especially at the end of the year. You can use this strategy to plug in your own "Shawn's" disruptive behavior and devise your own specific plan to change that behavior.

INDIVIDUAL STUDENT BEHAVIOR AND WORK CONTRACTS

If the strategy outlined above does not work, you may want to develop a more formal contract for specific students. Contracts can be an effective way to help students learn to manage their own behavior—to develop self-management, self-evaluation, and self-regulation skills. The first step is for the teacher and the student to discuss the problem and then draw up a contract that spells out the acceptable behavior (see Resource 4.2). Contracts work best if parents are informed and involved. Initially, both the teacher and student complete separate contracts and compare results. Students are praised for positive self-evaluations that match those given by the teacher. Discrepancies in teacher and student evaluations may suggest that the student is not accurately reporting her actions and requires more training. Over time, students should be able to accurately self-evaluate and complete the self-monitoring form.

It is important to understand that undesirable behavior often stems from feeling overwhelmed. When it comes to completing in-class assignments, some students simply cannot break down the individual steps involved in completing a larger task. These students often become frustrated and upset, resulting in negative behavior. Teaching students self-management strategies through the use of an individual work contract can greatly reduce negative behavior associated with feeling overwhelmed. (See Resource 4.3.)

As with the self-monitoring behavior contract, list the steps for completion of a given assignment. You may want to include a timeframe for completion of each step. Have students self-monitor their progress by checking a completion box after each step is completed. Initially, you may have students check in with you after each step is completed. Be sure to praise them for their efforts. Over time, you will want to teach students to self-reward when completing each step. Self-rewards may include getting a drink of water or three-to-five minutes of free-choice reading. Teach students to build endurance and perseverance by slowly "upping the ante." Make self-rewards contingent upon completion of several or all of the steps on the contract.

Additional strategies for helping students who appear overwhelmed by in-class assignments can include:

- Presenting materials individually—avoid giving work packets;
- Shortening assignments;
- Revealing only a few problems at a time—have students use a half sheet of paper to cover part of the page; and
- Offering peer-tutoring support—peers can offer immediate and specific feedback and support.

INCREASE POSITIVE INTERACTIONS

Although students with discipline problems need more positive feedback, they are likely to receive mostly negative feedback because of their misbehavior. Teachers of such students can easily fall into the trap of having mainly negative interactions with them. Negative interactions are emotionally draining for everyone involved. Constant criticism is damaging and drives a wedge between teachers and students. Teachers may even reach the point at which they have difficulty seeing the students' good qualities.

Try to increase positive interactions with your "behavior problems." The above example of teaching students to use a self-monitoring form forces teachers and students to focus on positive actions taken toward correcting inappropriate behavior.

Human nature is such that people often complain when something is wrong but say little when things are done right. It is often difficult to change to a more positive way of interacting. Ideally, you should try to get the rate of positive comments and interactions to between 50 percent and 75 percent of all comments given. This may feel difficult at first, but it will get easier and more natural with practice. You may wish to listen to and observe your own behavior toward your students for a day. Count how often you make positive statements. Can you find good reasons to smile at those exasperating children, make positive comments, praise, or give them a quick hug? "You did a great job cleaning up your desk." "Gee, you must be proud of the 87 you earned on your spelling test. You really studied. That's great. Keep up the good work." "The library corner looks so neat and organized. Thanks for picking it up!" In contrast, how many negative statements do you make? "I already explained that." "You will just have to stay in at recess." "Can't you just sit still and listen!" "The reason you don't get it is because you weren't paying attention."

Are your interactions mostly positive or negative? Teachers especially need to catch their "challenging" students being good and compliment the things they do well. If seat work has been a major problem, and your students start working on the assignment without being reminded, give them a pat on the shoulder, a smile, or a thanks immediately. Give kudos sincerely. Find at least some part of the job to commend. If compliments are too flowery, children may reject them. If you enthuse about schoolwork as if it were perfect and the students recognize that it is not, they may not respond at all positively to your interaction.

Plenty of people in the world are willing to tear down your "challenging" students by telling them they are bad, lazy, or wrong. Few people are willing to spend the extra time and energy required to be positive and build the children's self-esteem. It might take a strong conscious effort on your part to be as positive as possible. Make it your personal goal to fill these children's time in your classroom with positive interactions.

BE CONSISTENT

The most important principle of behavior management is consistency. Your students should always know what to expect if they behave in a certain way. To put it simply, they must understand that "good things happen when we behave appropriately, and there are consequences for when we don't."

One of the most difficult aspects of behavior management for new teachers (and many seasoned veterans) is to be consistent with the student discipline program every day—yes, even when you are tired and would love to pretend you didn't see that particular misbehavior. You must step in and promptly deal with it. You must constantly monitor what your students are doing. Use an "active eye." See what is going on. Avoid becoming preoccupied with someone or something and ignoring the rest of the class. It is said that one teacher on his feet is worth two in the seat. Staying on your feet benefits your discipline program.

Effective teachers feel confident and in charge of the situation in their classrooms. Perhaps most important, remember that in behavior management, your attitudes and expectations will act as self-fulfilling prophecies. Preventing discipline problems begins with the proactive attitude that you can and will promote respect and positive interactions in your classroom.

RESOURCE 4.1

Suggested Literature for Teaching Conflict Resolution in the Primary Classroom

Defining *Conflict Resolution*

Let's Be Enemies by Janice May Udry
Three Wishes by Lucille Clifton
The Honey Hunters by Francesca Martin
Stevie by Jon Steptoe
Swimmy by Leo Lionni
The Tale of Peter Rabbit by Beatrix Potter

The Escalation of Conflict

Matthew and Tilly by Rebecca C. Jones
The Owl and the Woodpecker by Brian Wildsmith
The Pig War by Betty Baker
It's Mine! by Leo Lionni
The Quarreling Book by Charlotte Zolotow

Conflict Solving Ideas

The Knight and the Dragon by Tomie de Paola
The Island of Skog by Steven Kellogg
Angel Child, Dragon Child by Michelle Maria Surat
Babar and the Wully-Wully by Lauren De Brunhoff
Clancy's Coat by Eve Bunting
First Pink Light by Eloise Greenfield
The Owl and the Woodpecker by Brian Wildsmith
The Pig War by Betty Baker
The Quarelling Book by Charlotte Zolotow
Who's in Rabbit's House? by V. Aardema
The Zax by Dr. Seuss
The Butter Battle Book by Dr. Seuss
Six Crows by Leo Lionni
The Terrible Thing That Happened at My House by Marge Blain
Bootsie Barker Bites by Barbara Bottner

Understanding Other Perspectives

The Hating Book by Charlotte Zolotow
Tar Beach by Faith Ringgold
Here Comes the Cat! by Frank Aschand Vladimir Vagin
Two Bad Ants by Chris Van Allsburg
The Chinese Mirror by Mirra Ginsburg
The True Story of the Three Pigs by Jon Scieszka

Conflict and Feelings

Spinky Sulks by William Steig
Alexander and the Terrible, Horrible, No Good, Very Bad Day by Judith Viorst
The Grouchy Ladybug by Eric Carle
The Teacher From the Black Lagoon by Mike Thayer
Grandpa's Face by Eloise Greenfield
The Little Brute Family by Russell Hoban

Caring, Respect, and Community

A Chair for My Mother by Vera Williams
Teammates by Peter Golenbock
Mufaro's Beautiful Daughter by Joh Steptoe
She Come Bringing Me That Little Baby Girl by Eloise Greenfield
Ty's One Man Band by Mildred Pitts Walter
Two Good Friends by Judy Delton
The Big Pile of Dirt by E. Clymer

RESOURCE 4.2

Sample Self-Monitoring Behavior Contract
for a Primary Student

Student Name: _____ Date: _____

Transitioning From Classroom to Recess

Did I remember to . . .

1. Walk?	Yes	No
2. Remain in line?	Yes	No
3. Keep my hands to myself?	Yes	No
4. Use a quiet voice?	Yes	No

My score: _____ /4

Observer's score: _____ /4

Number of matching yes scores: _____ /4

RESOURCE 4.3

Sample Individual Work Contract
for a Primary Student

Name: _____

Subject or Task: Multiplication Worksheet

Steps:	Check when completed:
1. First, answer all problems that are known (easy ones first).	☐
2. Second, try to solve unknown problems.	☐
3. If you are still having trouble with unknown problems, develop a specific question and ask a peer for assistance.	☐
4. Try to solve the remaining problems independently.	☐

5

Preparing Lesson Plans That Engage Students

PLANNING IS IMPORTANT!

Lesson planning is a critical part of effective teaching. Well-planned lessons have important consequences for both student learning and classroom behavior. The old adage "Failing to plan means planning to fail" is all too true in busy elementary classrooms. It is essential that you carefully and thoughtfully prepare for every minute with your students. Even a few minutes of unplanned time can result in unwieldy behavior from students!

Planning always takes more time than expected. It is a complex decision-making process that requires you to synthesize everything you have learned about teaching, such as models of instruction, cognitive and affective taxonomies, learning objectives, and lesson and unit design, and translate it into meaningful, standards-based lessons that meet the needs of your particular students. At the start of the year, it is wise to establish a dedicated time slot for your own lesson and classroom planning. By selecting specific days and times for your planning, you are less likely to run into scheduling conflicts that prevent you from getting your lessons ready. With a consistent planning schedule in place, you are more likely to enjoy some much needed down time and less likely to feel overwhelmed.

Decide when and where it is best for you to do your lesson planning: at school, during prep time, after school, or on weekends. Many new teachers enjoy a few quiet, uninterrupted hours on a weekend afternoon to get things done. Check the policy on using the building after work hours and on weekends. As a new teacher, you will require additional time to create or locate resources and materials for your lessons. You will also want to devote extra time to reviewing your plans carefully. Unlike experienced teachers, you will not have the benefit of having tried out particular lessons in previous years or of having materials made in advance. It may seem to you that your colleagues are able to plan quickly, and you may feel tempted to do the same. The truth is, much of their planning activities are hidden mental processes that are reflective, intuitive, and nonlinear, taking a large number of factors into consideration. At this stage of your career, your own planning must be more specific, careful, and detailed. Experience will gradually give you a better sense of how much to cover and how quickly, how to sequence material, how to start and end an activity, how to modify plans for individual children, and how to make changes if plans are not going as you expected.

In addition to your own individual planning time, check in with the other teachers at your grade level. Frequently, grade-level teams schedule weekly meetings to map out the week's lessons. If such a practice is not in place at your new school, ask a colleague if you can coplan weekly lessons and curriculum units. Offer to prepare materials or run copies of needed worksheets in exchange. Working together can really save time. Just remember, in the beginning, there are no shortcuts—plan to spend a lot of time planning.

Scope and Sequence of Lesson Planning

Once you have carved out a dedicated schedule for planning, the next step is to create a logical scope and sequence for your lessons. New teachers frequently report feeling only a day or two ahead of their students. You can prevent much of this undue stress by knowing where your lessons are going and what you will be teaching next. Effective lessons spiral and build from previous lessons. To accomplish this, you will want to begin by creating a master or long-range plan. A long-range plan is not a detailed plan; it is merely a road map of your instructional sequence for the year.

The first step in creating a long-range plan is to check existing state and school district documents listing the learning criteria for your grade level or subject. Your state department of education has published official curriculum frameworks outlining both content standards for each grade level as well as instructional profiles for designing and delivering instruction. Most school districts also have local curriculum guides, frameworks, or courses of study. These important resources, developed by teachers, outline what is to be taught and provide a clear sense of your district's expectations. Content standards typical for various grade levels are listed in Resource 5.1.

Once you have determined what skills and concepts you are required to teach, create a general month-by-month sequence for each content area. Carefully plan around months that are shortened by holidays and breaks. Also, consider grading periods. Some teachers map out long-range plans based on quarters or trimesters.

With the year mapped out, you are ready to develop more detailed short-range plans. This may include developing curriculum units.

Thinking of your curriculum as units of study allows you to integrate content areas, plan a broad array of learning activities, incorporate fieldtrips, and gather supplementary resources, including children's literature, interactive websites, web streaming videos, and more. Think about how one lesson interrelates with others in a unit. Children become more effective learners when you plan continuous, cohesive blocks of instruction that enable them to make connections among ideas. Individual lessons should flow into one another. Curriculum units typically span from three to six weeks in duration.

At this point, you are ready to begin planning individual lessons. In the busy elementary classroom, it is best to create a master plan for the week. Write in routine activities—attendance, recess, lunch, and breaks. Fill in your specialist schedule, including art, music, PE, library, computer lab, and any other specials. Now, you are ready to schedule the individual lessons that make up the overall unit of study.

Lesson Plan Design

Time is precious in the elementary classroom, so you want to make sure your lessons are effective and maximize student learning. While lesson plan outlines used in college teacher-preparation courses vary widely, the basic components are universal. The most effective lesson plans include the following elements:

1. Goals and objectives: What should the student be able to do, understand, or care about as a result of the lesson? Lesson objectives are taken directly from your state content standards and school or district curriculum guides.

2. Anticipatory set: Also referred to as the "hook" used to grab students' attention. The goal of the anticipatory set is to help students understand the relevance of the lesson and see the connection between the lesson objective and their own lives.

3. Establish and activate background knowledge: This is a critical step in an elementary classroom. Younger learners may not have the world experience or background knowledge needed to make connections and construct new knowledge. It is during this time that you create the context for the lesson. This is frequently done through the use of children's literature, pictures, videos, or any other realia and artifacts. This step is also critical for fostering language development of second-language learners.

4. Modeling: During this phase of the lesson, your job is to demonstrate what you expect students to accomplish. Explicitly show them how to accomplish the task in a step-by-step fashion. You will also want to share any mental strategies you use to complete the task or activity. This process is referred to as a "think aloud." Be sure to check for understanding throughout this phase of instruction. In addition to asking students to orally repeat the steps in the process, be sure to ask higher-order questions to probe for higher levels of understanding. Refer to Bloom's Taxonomy to develop higher-order questions. (See Resource 5.2.)

5. Guided practice: Give your students a chance to try out the activity with support. You may elect to have students work as partners or under your direct supervision. The goal is to ensure success before asking students to work independently.

6. Independent practice: Through independent and repeated practice, students work to master new skills. The overarching goal is for this skill set to become automatic and transfer to new and diverse learning contexts and not just the context in which it is initially learned.

7. Closure: This is another critical component of an effective lesson and a step frequently omitted by new teachers and veteran teachers alike. New teachers often find that lessons take longer than initially planned and therefore forego this aspect of the lesson. Be careful not to fall into this trap. You may need to allow more time for the lesson by extending it beyond a recess period or into the following day. Providing closure gives students the opportunity to make sense of what was just taught. During this time, you will want to restate learning objectives. Ask students to synthesize what they have learned and explain how they can use the skill in the future. Taking a few minutes at the close of each lesson to process the lesson will

   o Help students organize their learning;
   o Help students consolidate and synthesize learning;
   o Reinforce and clarify key points of the lesson; and
   o Create a bridge for subsequent lessons.

Some school administrators require teachers to submit lesson plans on a weekly basis. Regardless of whether this practice is required in your school, you will want to use this lesson plan outline as a framework as you prepare your lessons. You may want to keep a template handy during your first year. As time progresses and you gain more experience, you will internalize each component and begin to implement them intuitively.

Additional Considerations When Developing Lesson Plans

Below is a checklist of important questions to ask yourself when planning.

_____ 1. How will this lesson or unit be relevant to my students' lives?

_____ 2. Are the goals of this lesson or unit consistent with grade-level goals in my school district and/or state curriculum guides?

_____ 3. How will I make provisions for individual differences? Have I provided a variety of learning experiences to support all learning modalities and all types of learners?

_____ 4. Does this lesson or unit require my children to have prior knowledge and skills to complete it successfully?

_____ 5. Did I include enough vocabulary building for my students who have limited English? For my students with low reading levels? For my students with special needs?

_____ 6. Did I build from the concrete to the abstract? Does the lesson or unit follow a logical sequence?

_____ 7. How will my daily plan tie into my weekly, monthly, and yearly plans?

_____ 8. Is the content inclusive and at an appropriate depth?

_____ 9. What specific instructional strategies or activities do I intend to use?

_____10. In my lesson planning, have I considered not only the cognitive but also the affective domains? Are my lessons building morale and cohesion in my classroom?

_____11. Do I have all the resources I need, such as student materials, supplementary books, audiovisual materials, and speakers?

_____12. Have I tested all needed equipment to make sure it is operating correctly, such as computers, LCD projectors, or AVerVision or Elmo?

_____13. Have I bookmarked and previewed websites?

_____14. What procedures will I use to evaluate student learning?

Lesson Plan Basics

When it comes to selecting the goals and objectives for a particular lesson, stick to the old adage that "less is more." Two or three goals are plenty for one instructional sequence. When working with younger students, you may want to focus on even fewer goals. A common pitfall for new teachers is attempting to cover too much in a single lesson. While incidental learning will inevitably happen, focus your lesson on key learning outcomes. Keep in mind that student goals should be explicit, measureable, and stated in an active voice.

DISTRICT, STATE, AND NATIONAL STANDARDS

Implementing a Standards-Based Curriculum

Since the 2001 passage of No Child Left Behind (NCLB) mandating that *all* students meet or exceed national standards, most states have developed individual state curriculum frameworks. These frameworks include content standards as well as research-based approaches for effective instruction. Standards designate the explicit collection of the knowledge and skills students are expected to have at different stages of their education. This is great news for you as a new teacher because it has eliminated all the guesswork about what you should and should not be teaching. Before the implementation of national, state, and local standards, new teachers frequently had to rely on intuition or a collection of various materials garnered from other teachers when deciding what to teach. The current standards movement in education is aimed at alleviating situations in which curriculum content and teacher expectations for students in the same grade levels and same subjects vary greatly within and across buildings, districts, and states. Your state frameworks are an invaluable resource to you as you create your long-range plan, curriculum units, and individual lessons.

As a new teacher, you may encounter veteran teachers balking at or sharing frustrations regarding the implementation of a standards-based curriculum. Try not to let this influence your developing practice. Much of the stress educators feel during this time of educational reform is a result of accountability measures, namely standardized tests. While you will be expected to prepare students for and administer standardized tests on a yearly basis, try not to let this aspect of teaching affect your understanding of the purpose of standards. For more discussion on standardized testing, see Chapter 6.

In addition to learning the specific content standards required for your grade level, take time to become familiar with the standards required one grade above and one grade below the grade level you are teaching. Understanding this three-year range of learning expectations will enable you to modify your instruction for the individual needs of students in your class. This is a critical first step in differentiating instruction in a sequential and logical progression.

Materials and Resources

It's not necessary to reinvent the wheel each time you plan a lesson or unit. A vast number of commercial resources are available with thematic collections of lesson plans. Most of the more recently published materials are standards based. Before purchasing or using commercially prepared materials, check to see that they are aligned with the standards being implemented at your school. In addition to print materials, be sure to check publishers' websites. For instance, Teacher Created Materials (www.teachercreated.com) offers a wide variety of free, ready-to-use lesson plans and activities on their website. The plans are referenced to complete thematic units and complementary materials available for purchase if you wish. The Teacher Created Materials website also offers a Teachers' Forum with a Discussion Board to ask questions and share ideas, which includes a section called 1001+ Teacher Links—an extensive Internet database organized into categories, great for locating supplementary materials. Scholastic.com offers similar resources, as do most of the major publishers. Another personal favorite is the Discovery School website, which provides sections for teachers, students, and parents (you might want to mention it at your open house). The Teachers section offers a teacher-approved library of creative curriculum resources, including lesson plans, quizzes, puzzles, clip art, and Internet links to other resources.

You may also check educational catalogs and/or your local teacher supply store for additional lesson plan resources. Magazines such as *Instructor, Teaching K–8,* and *Learning* give ideas to incorporate into your lesson plans. Monthly teacher magazines contain many quick and easy tips, suggestions from teachers across the country, and current holiday activities.

Whatever the source of your lesson plans—the teacher's edition, another commercial source, the web, or your own creativity—you are likely to revise your initial plan after you've taught it. Use colored pens or markers to make comments about the lesson, what to do differently next time, and what worked especially well. Rarely in teaching can lesson plans be implemented again without some modification. Create a file of individual lessons and units that went particularly well. Include lesson plans, copies of student work samples, and photographs. Also, include a list of supplementary books used, websites, and any other resources. Don't trust your memory! Next year is a long way off, and you will be thankful for the resource.

Using Materials in the Teaching Manuals as a Guide

The elementary curriculum is crowded, and elementary teachers are expected to be masters of all content domains. Teacher manuals can be excellent tools to help you grasp the basic content of each subject and understand how this content is organized. Teacher manuals also include research-based activities, suggestions for learning experiences, and information about additional resources and readings to enhance your lessons.

School districts have regular adoptions of textbooks, usually in five- to seven-year cycles, so you should find that the materials you are expected to use are both up to date as well as standards based. Unfortunately, publishers have to create materials that align with the varying standards among states, so teacher manuals can be too comprehensive and therefore overwhelming. Your main job becomes making sure you understand the scope and sequence of the content for each subject and then choosing the most appropriate material and learning activities for your particular group of students.

Student textbooks, basal readers, and adopted instructional materials are not intended to displace the teacher's instructional decision making or to supplant opportunities for students to experience a wide range of learning activities. Think of your teacher manual as an instructional resource to help you provide basic, sequenced instruction for a wide variety of student abilities. Then, after sampling its contents, take control of your teacher manual so that it becomes only one resource among many for you as an informed and discriminating teacher.

Working From a Teacher Manual

1. First, read through an entire section or unit of the material to get a feel for the span and sequence. What are the main ideas?

2. What is your objective or purpose for presenting this particular lesson or unit? In some cases, you may not be able to use all the materials in the teacher manual. Do not expect to do everything suggested.

3. Make a list of teaching suggestions and materials related to your objectives. For instance, you might want all lessons to connect to a unit theme, such as the importance of sharing and helping family members. Generate ideas for lessons or activities that fit into this theme from a variety of additional sources: other teachers, community members, fiction and nonfiction books, poetry, real-life experiences, music, art, television, websites, and even billboards and advertisements.

4. Before using any of this material in a lesson plan, think about how it will enhance the learning and growth of your students. To ensure student learning and growth, take into account different learning aptitudes and styles; varied stages of readiness to learn; and the social, emotional, linguistic, cultural, cognitive, and intellectual needs of students.

5. Have available a short activity, story, graph, chart, picture, or video to help focus student attention and develop a readiness for the planned instruction. Once you have decided how to capture your

students' attention, consider how you will develop your lesson. Refer to your teacher manual for ideas. Then, ask yourself, "What else can I include?" To spark your creativity, here is a list of various instructional strategies, resources, and activities:

Book making	Independent projects	Posters
Bulletin boards	Individual packets	Problem solving
Cartooning	Interest centers	Puzzles
Characterizations	Interviews	Questioning strategies
Computers	Inventions	Rap sessions
Cooperative learning activities	Journal writing	Reference books
Debate	Magazines	Role-playing
Drama/puppets	Manipulatives	Skits
Field trips	Maps	Student-created board games
Films	Mind mapping	Team teaching
Flash cards	Mobiles	Technology projects
Games	Mock court	Video presentations
Graphs	Murals	Visualization
	Newspapers	

6. After considering various strategies and activities and choosing one or more for your lesson, try to visualize the actual instructional sequence:

    o Try to see what you and the students will be doing during the lesson. Imagine the lesson from different students' points of view.

    o Visualize the worst possible scenarios, too. Better yet, learn to anticipate. Do you really have enough glue and paint for each group of students? Suppose the students spill paint? What if unscheduled events or behavior problems interrupt plans? Activities that appear ideal in preplanning sometimes misfire. Given the multitude of variables in an elementary classroom, expect to modify and adapt your plans.

    o How will children share what they have learned and produced? Oral sharing, for instance, flows naturally from individual or group writing. If children finish early, how will you turn extra time at the end of a period into a productive learning experience?

Extending and Enriching the Basic Curriculum

Effective teachers go beyond the basic content or skills lessons of the official adopted curriculum and encourage students to do the same. Enrichment activities extend content to related personal interests, pertinent topics, or relevant skills.

Here are a few examples of curriculum enrichment:

• Regardless of the grade you teach, read to your students every day. If you are unsure where to begin, a list of outstanding read-aloud books is provided in Resource 5.3. Read alouds expand children's understanding of the world around them. Set aside one specific time each day for a story. Read alouds can enhance your unit themes, but you do not have to tie every book to class work. Allow time for discussion after reading. Your students will look forward to the story if you read one or two chapters at a time and then invite them to predict what will happen next. Read with plenty of expression, slowly enough for each child to build mental pictures.

- Invite your students to choose two favorite stories. Ask the children to imagine what would happen if the character in one story found herself in the second story's setting and had to solve a different problem.

- Small groups of students can choose a favorite author, artist, or musician and then obtain information about that person's life and works. If students choose persons who lived a long time ago, ask them to find world events that their persons might have seen, heard about, or even helped to influence.

- Introduce a new word each day, and challenge your students to include it in one of their stories, use it in conversation at least once, and explore its origins and other definitions. For example, do origins of this word include another language or incorporate a slang term?

- Add an oral language component to your lessons, such as brain storming, discussing, or dramatization. Build in time for natural oral interaction, collaborative small-group talking, writing, editing, and sharing.

- Take advantage of opportunities for students to participate in hands-on activities. In science, for example, students may be able to test their own hypotheses in an activity or experiment. Scientific concepts are not simply passed down by the teacher and absorbed ready made by the children. Allow students to demonstrate ideas they have learned, do experiments based on content read, and solve problems embedded in information uncovered.

- Collect and recycle throwaway items, such as empty containers, into useful classroom teaching aids, musical instruments, arts and crafts materials, and toys. Encourage students and parents to help you collect needed items.

- Challenge your students to solve nonroutine math problems, such as soma cubes (seven puzzle pieces that can be assembled into a three-inch-by-three-inch cube) and Rubik's Cube, and then explain how each puzzle was solved.

- Encourage children to keep a learning log as part of content-area study and/or a literature response journal as they read short stories, novels, and poems. They can write in their logs or journals on topics of their own choosing or in response to such questions as these:
  - What is the main idea or theme?
  - How does this idea develop in the selection?
  - What does this idea mean to you personally?
  - When have you ever experienced something similar?

- Children enjoy painting or drawing pictures based on their readings and learnings. They can make an illustration to accompany the reading selection. Illustrations may be maps, charts, graphs, or tables, as well as artistic renderings. Invite them to orally share their illustrations.

Share a piece of classical music that relates to the mood or theme of a story. Discuss the relationships.

- Students can construct something based on their readings or content-area study—a diorama, a model, a bulletin board, a PowerPoint or Key Note presentation, or a timeline. They can also respond with a form of drama, such as monologue, dialogue, role-playing, choral reading or speaking, and a Reader's Theater rendition that relates to the content read or learned.

Be brave about trying new strategies and materials. Continue to search for ways to improve your lessons. Planning and implementing great lessons takes time, but your extra effort will prove worthwhile.

TIME ON TASK

In addition to careful researching and planning of instructional activities, you must also give close attention to how you will use classroom *time*. What is the connection between learning time and student learning and growth? Two major findings have emerged.

1. Students' achievement is higher when they spend more time engaged in learning activities (e.g., practicing skills, discussing, problem solving, and reading).

2. The amount of time students spend learning differs dramatically from classroom to classroom.

The Northwest Regional Educational Laboratory (1986) reported that in one fifth-grade reading class, for example, students were observed to engage in reading activities 120 hours during the year. Students in a comparable classroom spent 298 hours on reading—two-and-one-half times more than the other students! Achievement test scores reflected this difference.

In fifth-grade classes, time spent on reading varied from an average of 27 minutes a day to an average of 53 minutes a day. Which children do you think showed greater reading achievement and aptitude?

In one state, second graders are supposed to learn fractions. But, a study found that second-grade classrooms actually spent from 0 to 399 minutes during the year on fractions, depending on their teacher.

What Is Engaged Time?

Is engaged time the time the school has scheduled for instruction? The time the teacher devotes? Or, is it the time students actually spend engaged in learning tasks? Just looking at a schedule will not tell you how much work a class really does—or how any one student has spent the time. A schedule gives only the broad, official version of how much time every student spends learning a subject. By scheduling or devoting more time for a subject, you can increase your students' opportunity to learn. But, scheduling and teaching do not guarantee that students are actually *attending* to the learning activity.

Engaged time is the essence of classroom learning. It is the amount of time your students actually work on any assigned activity that builds the desired skill—for example, working on written assignments, actively discussing a problem in a cooperative learning group, reading silently, and listening carefully as you explain a subject. It can include reading aloud or rapid-fire drill and practice of math facts. Engaged time will vary from student to student as well as from class to class.

In a school year of the same number of days, students with an efficient and effective teacher receive the equivalent of many more days' instruction than do those unfortunate children in classrooms in which many minutes each day are wasted. If you eliminate wasted time during transitions, during instruction, and after instruction, not only will discipline problems lessen, but substantial gains in academic learning time will be realized.

Not all your classroom time can be spent in dynamic learning, of course. Some nonacademic time is needed—taking roll, for example, or moving from one task to the next. Some off-task behavior by students is inevitable. Good teaching does not imply that students should be engaged in academic learning every moment they are in school. However, too much nonengaged time interferes with learning in many classes.

Think about your own classroom during reading or math time. How much time will your students spend getting ready or straightening up? Do they need to wait for your attention? Do some of them daydream? Do they socialize or watch what others are doing? Do they get restless before the end of the scheduled period? How much time is expended waiting for class to start, waiting for the reading group to gather, waiting for papers to be passed out or collected, waiting to be dismissed? All this waiting leaves students with nothing to do but entertain themselves. Usually, they fill this time by talking, playing with friends, or getting into trouble. Additional valuable time is lost as you endeavor to regain students' attention and refocus students for the next learning. Pay close attention to how your students use time in your classroom. Resources 5.4 and 5.5 are forms to help you plan and assess your classroom time on task.

The importance of time on task has been well documented for the past 20 years. One of the first studies of beginning teachers in California (Fisher et al., 1978), for instance, showed the importance of maintaining high-engagement rates. When teachers allocated and spent more classroom time on a specific topic, their students learned more in that area. Engagement rate (the percentage of allocated time that students were engaged) was shown to be directly related to student learning. Differences in time on task are important. Students who receive less instruction are still expected to do well on the standardized tests given at the end of the year and are compared with students whose teachers maintained high-engagement time. In fairness to your students, you must maximize allocated time on academic subjects and manage your classroom so that students are engaged, on task, and achieving success.

PLANNING INTEGRATED UNITS

Effective elementary teachers integrate curriculum as much as possible. They realize that integrated units help students synthesize information and transfer knowledge across discipline areas. Children become more effective learners when their teachers have planned continuous, cohesive blocks of instruction. This approach differs from the traditional approach of teaching separate subjects at different times in the school day. In an integrated curriculum, subjects are intermeshed, and instructional strategies are used that actively involve students. Cooperative learning, project-based learning, peer tutoring, inquiry, schema theory, and recent models of the brain and learning all find a natural home in curriculum integration. Children communicate actively with one another, make connections among ideas, and think critically and creatively. Recent research indicates that this type of teaching can lead to high levels of thinking and significant learning. It can also lead to enthusiasm and high-engagement rates.

Units are integrated, cohesive blocks of experiences in which individual lessons flow into one another. Many natural opportunities are provided for children to listen, speak, read, write, and think. Instructional variety is central to an integrated curriculum. Although you plan integrated units carefully, you generally allow choices and open-ended projects in this type of teaching. Unit teaching enables you to individualize the curriculum to meet diverse learning needs.

The simplest way to plan integrated units is to focus on a topic. Pets, holidays, seasons, whales, bears, monsters, chocolate, and dragons are common topics in primary classrooms. It is relatively easy to find children's literature (fiction, poems, and nonfiction) that relates to these topics and then to extend the learning experiences into science, social studies, art, music, and perhaps even math activities. A word of caution however, the topical approach to unit design can be superficial. Students may have difficulty understanding how to transfer information from one content area to another. You too may also find it challenging to create meaningful connections between and among the content areas. All too often, activities are selected simply because they fit the topic rather than addressing a standard in a meaningful way.

Another common type of integrated unit is thematic: Learning experiences are developed based on a common theme, message, or idea that underlies the study. The theme explains the significance of the study—it tells the students what the experience means. Look to your teacher manuals for suggested themes. Science, history, social science, as well as character education curriculum contain a myriad of themes relevant to the elementary classroom.

Often, a thematic unit is built around literature that demonstrates the theme at its core. Children read the same selections together or alone, as well as additional books, articles, and poems. Experiences in music and art, as well as science and social studies, are part of the exploration of the theme. In some schools, all the teachers at a grade level collaborate on a common theme and its content.

Once you have decided on a topic or theme, you design a unit much as you plan a lesson—identifying objectives; choosing literature that will focus the theme; deciding on the listening, speaking, reading, writing, science, art, music, and physical activities that will be part of the unit; looking for cross-curricular connections; deciding on your means of assessing students' progress toward your unit's objectives; and planning an opening celebration to begin the class's journey. Then, you are ready to plan the specific lessons within the unit, including how you will group students and for which activities. See Resources 5.6 and 5.7 for helpful unit planning forms.

In planning an integrated unit, you may likely find that your basal reading series contains literacy selections grouped as units. In this case, you may decide to adapt the ideas and selections in the series. Maybe you would rather begin the unit with a poem or story of your own choosing or have upper elementary students read the original, full-length version of a novel rather than the excerpted one. Keep in mind the lesson planning ideas discussed earlier in this chapter. It is unnecessary to require children to read every piece in the basal unit. Choose what meets the needs of your students. Add and delete. Skip selections and rearrange the order. You may even decide to skip an entire unit in the basal reader and substitute an alternate unit you build yourself.

Curriculum Planning for Multicultural Classrooms

Depending on the grade level you teach, you can infuse multicultural education into the basic curriculum by using one or more of the following approaches. In the *single-group approach,* you teach a unit that provides a great deal of information on a certain culture, for example, Mexicans, Native Americans, or Chinese. In the *topical approach,* you present or allow students to present information about one aspect of a given culture, such as its holidays, legends, music, heroes, tall tales, art, houses, and so on.

Both these approaches, although interesting to students and commonly used by teachers, have potential problems. Often referred to as the "holidays and heroes approach," the *single-group* and *topical approaches* can paint a simplistic and superficial portrayal of a culture or a way of life. For this reason, the *conceptual* approach is considered the most comprehensive. The conceptual approach incorporates such concepts as communications, language, and cultural patterns (beliefs, customs, and rituals) into your lessons in various subject areas, such as language arts and social studies. For example, what legends are similar in many countries (e.g., Cinderella and Little Red Riding Hood)? How do different countries all use the same food (e.g., rice)? Your objective is to incorporate cultural studies as part of the daily life in your classroom. In this approach, you are careful not to represent culture as just "food and fun" (holidays and celebrations). Make sure pictures in instructional materials show people's daily life rather than just special celebrations. Focus on how people are all the same in many ways rather than just looking at differences.

PLANNING INSTRUCTION AND DESIGNING LEARNING EXPERIENCES FOR *ALL* CHILDREN

Making good decisions about instruction is a complex and demanding process. As an effective teacher, you will plan lessons and units with your students in mind. You will design instruction to respond to individual learners and individual learning modalities. The richness of student diversities will be reflected in your planning. As an effective teacher, you will ensure high levels of student engagement and set high expectations for the success of each child in your class. You know that good instructional planning starts with the goals established by the school district or state, and then it meets and surpasses them!

RESOURCE 5.1

An Overview of Learning Objectives for Elementary Students

INTRODUCTION

These objectives are representative of basic learning expectations in language arts, reading, and mathematics at Grades 1, 3, and 5. This composite set of objectives was derived from several sets developed in school districts in the state of Washington, but the expected learnings are typical of what is required throughout the United States.

Use this overview as a reference to focus your instruction. If your school or district has provided a similar list, refer to it instead. For more information when you want to explore, understand, and use the standards and benchmarks that have been developed in all the major content areas, an excellent reference is *Content Knowledge: A Compendium of Standards and Benchmarks for K–12 Education* by John Kendall and Robert Marzano (1996). This reference was developed by the Mid-Continent Regional Educational Laboratory and is available from the Association for Supervision and Curriculum Development (toll free 1–800–933–ASCD; also available on CD-ROM). This 610-page resource has more than two hundred and fifty standards and 4,800 benchmarks organized into three broad categories of knowledge (procedural, declarative, and contextual knowledge), making it possible to identify targets for learning at every grade level.

It is often worthwhile to carefully review the objectives for the grade level just below and above yours. Know where your students have been academically and where they are expected to go when they leave your classroom.

FIRST GRADE

Language Arts, First-Grade Learning Objectives

In a language arts program, all students should receive instruction and practice in writing, speaking, and listening. The curriculum enables students to communicate skillfully, to listen critically, to write and speak effectively, and to think logically and creatively. Language arts skills spiral through the grades, with each level expanding on previous skills and experiences. Major instructional topics and student objectives include the following:

A. Composition Skills

The student understands that writing is a process that involves several steps: prewriting, writing, revision, and presenting.

1. Writes for a specific purpose and audience

2. Writes complete sentences

3. Uses editing skills

B. Handwriting Skills
1. Forms manuscript letters correctly
2. Demonstrates proper size, spacing, and appropriate speed
3. Demonstrates neatness in printing

C. Language Study Skills
1. Recognizes a sentence as expressing a complete thought
2. Develops skill in using nouns, adjectives, and verbs
3. Uses capital letters for first word in a sentence, *I* used as a pronoun, and proper nouns
4. Uses correct punctuation at the end of a statement or question
5. Recognizes correct verb tense
6. Recognizes correct subject and verb agreement

D. Listening Skills
1. Listens attentively at appropriate times
2. Follows oral one- and two-step directions in sequence
3. Practices common directional clue words (e.g., *first, last, next, left,* and *right*)
4. Listens to paragraphs and stories and identifies
   a. Important details
   b. Topics
   c. Main ideas
   d. Predicted outcomes
5. Identifies correct sequence of events

E. Reference and Study Skills
1. Reads for information
2. Begins to use alphabetical order
3. Categorizes words and ideas into similar groups

F. Speaking Skills
1. Speaks with clarity and appropriate voice control
2. Focuses on a topic
3. Answers questions in complete sentences
4. Participates in show-and-tell/group discussion

G. Spelling Skills
1. Spells words at first-grade level
2. Learns weekly lists of words
3. Uses assigned spelling words correctly in sentences
4. Applies spelling generalizations (rules)

Reading, First-Grade Learning Objectives

An elementary reading program is designed to develop competent readers who read for information and pleasure. Decoding, comprehension, and literary skills are developed through a variety of instructional approaches. Major instructional topics and student objectives include the following:

A. Decoding Skills

1. Distinguishes alphabetic letter forms
   a. Recognizes similarities and differences between upper- and lower-case letters
   b. Identifies upper- and lowercase letters by name
   c. Recognizes vowels and consonants
2. Distinguishes letter-sound associations
3. Distinguishes beginning sounds and letters
4. Distinguishes ending sounds and letters
5. Substitutes initial and final consonants
6. Discriminates short and long vowel sounds
7. Uses picture clues to decode unfamiliar words
8. Uses sentence context to decode unfamiliar words
9. Recognizes letter blends (clusters) in initial and final position
10. Distinguishes digraphs in initial and final position (*sh, ch, th, ck, kn,* and *wh*)
11. Recognizes the addition of *-s, -ing, -ed, -or,* and *-er* to base (root) words
12. Recognizes the addition of *-s* or *-es* to indicate plural
13. Recognizes the addition of *-'s* to nouns to indicate possession
14. Understands spelling generalizations
    a. When action words end in a single consonant following a short vowel, the final consonant is usually doubled before adding *-ed* or *-ing*
    b. When action words end with a final *e,* that *e* is usually dropped before adding a suffix that begins with a vowel
    c. When action words end in *y,* that *y* is usually changed to *i* before adding a suffix that begins with a vowel
15. Identifies base words
16. Understands contractions as two words combined with an apostrophe representing one or more omitted letters
17. Identifies vowel combinations and their sounds
18. Differentiates between hard and soft sounds of *c* and *g*
19. Recognizes compound words as two combined words
20. Identifies a suffix as a common syllable added to the end of a word
21. Identifies a prefix as a common syllable added to the beginning of a word

B. Comprehension Skills

1. Derives word meaning from picture context clues
2. Distinguishes among multiple word meanings

3. Identifies word referents (pronouns)

4. Recognizes and interprets punctuation (. ? ! " " ,)

C. Literary Skills

1. Reads for enjoyment

2. Demonstrates beginning library use skills

Mathematics, First-Grade Learning Objectives

A mathematics program should strive to give all students instruction in skills, applications, and concepts. The process of developing thoughtful behavior in mathematics requires that, throughout the grades and within each strand, instruction should progress from the concrete level, through pictorial representation, to abstract symbolization.

Problem solving, rather than exercises, should be the mainstay of instruction and learning. Students should apply their mathematical skills and understanding, inquiry skills, and thinking skills to formulate and solve problems.

Major instructional topics and student objectives include the following:

A. Place Value and Counting

1. Recognizes 0 to 20 objects

2. Recognizes number words *zero* to *ten*

3. Reads and writes numerals 0 to 100

4. Counts by ones, fives, and tens to one hundred

5. Identifies ordinal numbers 1st through 10th

6. Understands place values of 10s and 1s to 100

7. Counts on and back

8. Determines which numeral comes before, after, or between to compare numbers 1 to 20

B. Adding Whole Numbers

1. Adds two- and three-digit numbers

2. Estimates sums

3. Understands addition as a joining process

4. Understands sums through 18

5. Adds quantities of money using pennies, nickels, dimes, and quarters

6. Solves addition problems using horizontal and vertical forms

C. Subtracting Whole Numbers

1. Understands subtraction as a separating process

2. Demonstrates knowledge of the mental math techniques of counting back one, two, or three to find differences

3. Uses mental math technique of subtracting with zero

4. Memorizes facts to 12

5. Solves subtraction problems using horizontal and vertical forms

      6. Uses mental math technique of subtracting nine and subtracting doubles to find differences

      7. Understands add-to-check fact to subtract

  D. Fractions

      1. Identifies equal parts of a whole unit

      2. Recognizes 1/2, 1/3, and 1/4

  E. Problem Solving and Applications

      1. Collects and organizes data

      2. Reads a bar graph and pictograph

      3. Uses a variety of data sources to solve a problem (data sources may include information from a story, chart, table, or graph)

      4. Understands how to choose the operation that fits a given problem

      5. Determines reasonable estimates

      6. Uses pictures of coins (penny, nickel, dime, and quarter) to solve problems

      7. Determines whether answers to problems are reasonable

  F. Critical Thinking and Logic

      1. Identifies number, color, and position patterns

      2. Understands sorting and classification by attributes

      3. Compares and contrasts attributes

      4. Demonstrates use of critical thinking to identify differences

  G. Measurement

      1. Estimates and measures length using a ruler to measure inches and feet

      2. Estimates and measures using a centimeter ruler

      3. Estimates, measures, and compares weight

THIRD GRADE

Language Arts, Third-Grade Learning Objectives

  A. Composition Skills

    The student understands that writing is a process that involves several steps: prewriting, writing, revision, and presenting.

      1. Writes for a specific purpose and audience

      2. Writes a paragraph using at least three related sentences

      3. Uses correct form to write a personal letter

      4. Uses editing skills

  B. Handwriting Skills

      1. Writes using correct manuscript form, spacing, and size

      2. Reviews lowercase cursive letters and joining strokes taught in second grade

3. Writes uppercase cursive letters
4. Uses margins, titles, headings, and indentations correctly
5. Practices good penmanship habits and skills

C. Language Study Skills

1. Writes complete declarative, interrogative, and exclamatory sentences and uses correct ending punctuation
2. Uses capital letters for first word in a sentence, *I* used as a pronoun, and proper nouns
3. Identifies nouns, pronouns, verbs, and adjectives
4. Uses correct verb tense
5. Practices correct subject and verb agreement
6. Identifies subject and predicate
7. Writes abbreviations and initials correctly
8. Uses comma for date, city, state, and series of items
9. Uses colon for writing time of day
10. Identifies apostrophe for writing contractions and possessives
11. Uses *a* and *an* correctly
12. Uses subjective pronouns correctly (*I, we, you, he, she, it,* and *they*)

D. Listening Skills

1. Listens at appropriate times
2. Follows one-, two-, and three-step oral directions
3. Practices listening carefully and responding to others in a group discussion
4. Listens to an oral presentation for important details, topic, main ideas, and predicted outcomes

E. Reference and Study Skills

1. Alphabetizes to the third letter
2. Uses guide words to locate entry words in a dictionary
3. Uses alphabetical order for reference in
   a. Dictionary
   b. Glossary
4. Understands key information found on title page
5. Uses table of contents to locate information

F. Speaking Skills

1. Strives for appropriate expression when reading aloud
2. Practices speaking with clarity and appropriate voice control
3. Gives informal talks and oral presentations
4. Participates in group discussion
5. Focuses on topic of discussion

G. Spelling Skills

   1. Spells words at third-grade level

   2. Learns weekly lists of words

   3. Applies spelling generalizations (rules) in written work

   4. Spells words correctly from dictated sentences

   5. Proofreads for spelling errors

Reading, Third-Grade Learning Objectives

A. Decoding Skills

   1. Demonstrates ability to use skills taught in first and second grade, including

     a. Distinguishing letter-sound associations

     b. Distinguishing short and long vowel sounds

     c. Recognizing the addition of *-s* or *-es* to indicate plural

     d. Using context and picture clues

     e. Recognizing base words

     f. Recognizing common syllables (prefixes and suffixes)

     g. Recognizing compound words

     h. Recognizing consonant clusters (blends) and digraphs

     i. Recognizing the function of an apostrophe in contractions and possessives

   2. Determines the number of syllables in a word

   3. Applies syllabication rules to divide two-syllable words

   4. Recognizes synonyms, antonyms, and homonyms

B. Comprehension Skills

   1. Demonstrates ability to use skills taught in first and second grade, including

     a. Following oral and printed directions

     b. Understanding sequential order

     c. Remembering important details

     d. Recognizing multiple meanings of words

     e. Categorizing groups of like words

     f. Understanding that a pronoun may refer to a noun in a previous sentence or in the same sentence

     g. Deriving meaning from punctuation marks (. ? ! — , . . . " " :)

     h. Identifying the topic and/or main idea of a paragraph or story

     i. Drawing conclusions and making inferences

     j. Predicting outcomes

     k. Recognizing cause-effect relationships

2. Derives additional meaning from punctuation
   a. Commas for added emphasis
   b. Italics for emphasis
3. Uses dictionary and glossary to locate information
4. Draws appropriate conclusions
5. Distinguishes cause-effect relationships
6. Recognizes supporting detail

C. Literary Skills
   1. Distinguishes between fiction and nonfiction
   2. Distinguishes between fantasy and realistic fiction and between fact and opinion
   3. Recognizes elements of story
      a. Character
      b. Setting
   4. Recognizes various types of literature: stories, plays, poems, and informational articles

Mathematics, Third-Grade Learning Objectives

A. Place Value and Counting
   1. Demonstrates ability to use skills taught in first and second grade, including
      a. Identifying 1s, 10s, 100s, and 1,000s place
      b. Counting by ones to 999 and writing standard numerals
      c. Counting by 2s, 3s, 4s, 5s, 10s, and 25s
      d. Using ordinal numbers to the 10th place to indicate position in line
      e. Comparing numbers (greater than, less than)
   2. Develops understanding of negative numbers
   3. Rounds numbers to the nearest 10 and/or 100

B. Adding Whole Numbers
   1. Demonstrates ability to use skills taught in second grade, including
      a. Addition facts through 18 memorized
      b. Finding missing addends in basic addition problems
      c. Adding three or more single-digit numerals without regrouping
      d. Adding two-digit numerals with regrouping from 1s to 10s
      e. Estimating sums
   2. Develops understanding of the properties of whole numbers and addition
   3. Adds three- and four-digit numerals with regrouping in two places

C. Subtracting Whole Numbers
1. Demonstrates ability to use skills taught in second grade, including
   a. Subtraction facts through 18 memorized
   b. Subtracting two-digit numerals with regrouping from 10s to 1s
   c. Developing mental math techniques (counting up, fact families)
2. Develops understanding of the properties of subtraction
3. Subtracts three-digit numerals with regrouping in two places
4. Estimates differences

D. Multiplying Whole Numbers
1. Demonstrates ability to use skills taught in second grade, including
   a. Understanding multiplication as repeated addition process
   b. Using objects to find the product of two numerals (5 or less)
2. Develops understanding of the properties of multiplication
3. Completes related multiplication sentences for basic facts through $9 \times 9 = 81$
4. Memorizes basic multiplication facts through $9 \times 9 = 81$
5. Multiplies by a two-digit numeral without regrouping
6. Multiplies by a two-digit numeral with regrouping

E. Dividing Whole Numbers
1. Understands division as sharing or separating to make equal groups
2. Perceives the relationship of multiplication to division
3. Completes related division sentences for basic facts through $81 \div 9 = 9$
4. Uses two-digit quotients and one-digit divisors with remainders

F. Fractions
1. Demonstrates ability to use skills taught in second grade, including
   a. Writing a fraction to identify part of a whole
   b. Writing a fraction to identify part of a set of objects
   c. Finding a fraction of a number
2. Compares and orders fractions
3. Computes with fractions and mixed numbers
4. Adds and subtracts like denominators
5. Converts decimals and fractions

G. Problem Solving and Applications
1. Demonstrates ability to use skills taught in second grade, including
   a. Solving problems using the following strategies:
      o Missing data
      o Making a list
      o Looking for patterns
      o Guessing and checking
      o Using logical reasoning

   o Drawing a picture
   o Acting it out
  b. Determining reasonableness of answers by estimation
 2. Chooses correct operation to solve word problems

H. Geometry
 1. Demonstrates ability to use skills taught in second grade, including
  a. Identifying, sorting, and making solid figures
  b. Drawing and making plane figures
  c. Identifying and making symmetric and congruent figures
 2. Identifies plane and space figures
 3. Develops understanding of patterns, symmetry, and congruency

I. Measurement, Time, and Money
 1. Demonstrates ability to use skills taught in second grade, including
  a. Identifying quarter and half-dollar
  b. Finding the value of a collection of coins, including pennies, nickels, dimes, and quarters (total less than $1.00)
  c. Measuring with nonstandard units
  d. Measuring to the nearest inch and centimeter
  e. Measuring weight with pounds
  f. Measuring mass with kilograms
  g. Measuring capacity with cups, pints, quarts, and liters
  h. Reading thermometers (Fahrenheit)
  i. Beginning to tell time to nearest five-minute interval
 2. Develops understanding of perimeter, area, weight, and volume
 3. Compares units of temperature
 4. Measures to nearest half-inch using inch, foot, and yard
 5. Recognizes centimeter and meter as linear measures
 6. Tells time from the hour to one-minute interval
 7. Finds the value of a collection of coins (less than $2.00) and records the amount using correct symbols
 8. Adds, subtracts, multiplies, and divides money

J. Decimals
 1. Understands place value
 2. Compares and orders decimals
 3. Adds and subtracts decimals
 4. Converts decimals and fractions
 5. Rounds decimals
 6. Relates decimals to money

K. Consumer Math
 1. Applies mathematical knowledge in shopping and travel situations

  L. Critical Thinking and Logic

   1. Demonstrates ability to use skills taught in first and second grade, including

    a. Predicting and verifying

    b. Evaluating evidence and conclusions

    c. Classifying and sorting

    d. Comparing and contrasting

    e. Using spatial visualization

    f. Making generalizations

   2. Understands patterns

   3. Develops spatial visualization and logical reasoning

   4. Evaluates and generalizes

  M. Algebra

   1. Understands and uses variables and equations

   2. Develops knowledge of patterns, functions, relations, and algebraic expressions

  N. Data Collection and Analysis

   1. Collects and records data

   2. Makes graphs

   3. Makes questionnaires and tally charts

   4. Takes surveys and summarizes results

  O. Statistics and Problem Solving

   1. Collects data

   2. Presents data graphically

   3. Makes choices based on probability

   4. Makes predictions

  P. Graphs and Graphing

   1. Demonstrates ability to use skills taught in first and second grade, including

    a. Making and using bar graphs

    b. Reading pictographs

   2. Uses various graphing methods

FIFTH GRADE

Language Arts, Fifth-Grade Learning Objectives

  A. Composition Skills

  The student understands that writing is a process that may involve several steps: prewriting, writing, revising, and presenting.

   1. Writes for a specific purpose and audience

   2. Writes a topic sentence

3. Constructs paragraphs
4. Writes concluding statements
5. Writes on a given topic
6. Writes specific types of poetry
7. Writes dialogue
8. Writes paragraphs from notes
9. Organizes information
10. Lists sources of information
11. Uses editing skills
12. Writes and uses correct form of personal letter
13. Begins writing business letter in correct form

B. Handwriting Skills
   1. Continues to demonstrate proper shape of letters
   2. Demonstrates uniform slant
   3. Leaves adequate margins
   4. Begins papers with proper headings

C. Language Study Skills
   1. Identifies the following parts of speech
      a. Nouns
      b. Verbs
      c. Pronouns
      d. Adjectives, adverbs, and prepositions
      e. Conjunctions
   2. Uses correct verb tense and form
   3. Identifies forms of the verb *to be*
   4. Identifies noun and verb phrases
   5. Practices rules for capitalization
   6. Practices rules for punctuation
   7. Refines proofreading skills

D. Listening Skills
   1. Derives meaning from listening to oral reading of various forms of literature
   2. Understands oral directions
   3. Demonstrates appropriate etiquette as part of an audience
   4. Takes notes from oral information

E. Reference and Study Skills
   1. Uses library card catalog
   2. Demonstrates dictionary skills by locating words and interpreting pronunciation keys
   3. Locates and uses index

4. Locates and uses table of contents

5. Uses encyclopedia to locate information

6. Takes notes from written material

7. Begins to summarize information

F. Speaking Skills

1. Reads with appropriate interpretation and expression

2. Answers specific questions

3. Speaks on a topic for a specific purpose

4. Recites poetry

G. Spelling Skills

1. Spells words at the fifth-grade level

2. Learns weekly lists of words

3. Applies spelling generalizations

4. Writes spelling words from dictation

5. Proofreads for spelling errors

Reading, Fifth-Grade Learning Objectives

A. Decoding Skills

1. Uses prefixes, suffixes, and base words

2. Applies pronunciation rules

3. Uses accent marks

4. Uses dictionary pronunciation key

B. Comprehension Skills

1. Uses context clues

2. Differentiates between facts and opinions

3. Follows directions in sequence

4. Identifies cause-effect relationships

5. Draws conclusions

6. Notes details

7. Uses glossary and dictionary for word meanings

8. Derives meaning from idioms, metaphors, and similes

9. Recognizes main idea of paragraphs

10. Identifies topic sentence

11. Uses clue words to establish sequence

C. Literary Skills

1. Recognizes types of literature

a. Biography

b. Autobiography

      c. Fiction

      d. Nonfiction

      e. Fantasy

  2. Identifies main and minor characters

  3. Distinguishes between narrative and dialogue

  4. Recognizes plot

  5. Identifies point of view

  6. Describes setting

  7. Identifies story elements

Mathematics, Fifth-Grade Learning Objectives

A. Place Value and Counting

  1. Uses critical thinking to find number patterns

  2. Understands the meaning of place value through millions

  3. Rounds numbers to the nearest 1,000 or 10,000

  4. Recognizes concept of one billion

  5. Explores algebra by evaluating algebraic expressions with one variable

B. Multiplying Whole Numbers

  1. Divides three- and four-digit numerals by one- and two-digit divisors with and without zeros in the quotient

C. Fractions

  1. Uses the concept of least common multiple to determine the least common denominator

  2. Changes fractions to simplest forms or lowest terms

  3. Adds fractions with and without like denominators

  4. Subtracts fractions with and without like denominators

  5. Adds mixed numerals with and without regrouping

  6. Subtracts mixed numerals with and without regrouping

  7. Multiplies a fraction by a fraction

D. Decimals

Most mathematics programs integrate decimals with whole numbers for all operations.

  1. Recognizes decimals to thousandths

  2. Practices adding and subtracting decimals

  3. Begins to multiply by hundredths

  4. Divides a decimal by a whole numeral

  5. Rounds decimals to the nearest whole numeral or thousandth place

E. Problem Solving and Applications

Most math programs integrate critical thinking, problem solving, and math reasoning into every major unit of instruction.

1. Solves story problems using one or more whole number operations

2. Solves problems using measurements drawn to scale

3. Solves computer and calculator problems

F. Geometry

1. Identifies and measures acute, right, and obtuse angles

2. Investigates, identifies, and measures perimeter, area, and volume of common types of triangles, quadrilaterals, polygons, and circles

G. Measurement: Customary and Metric

1. Recognizes millimeter as unit of measurement

2. Adds and subtracts linear measures using fractions to the nearest sixteenth of an inch or to the nearest millimeter

3. Understands, calculates, and uses appropriate units of measurement for linear distance, area, volume, weight, time, and temperature

H. Ratios and Percentages

1. Solves proportions

2. Writes ratios/fractions as percentages and vice versa

3. Finds percentages of a number

I. Probability

1. Finds probability of equally likely outcomes

2. Conducts experiments to compare experimental with mathematical probability

3. Uses critical thinking and simulations to predict possible outcomes

RESOURCE 5.2

Using Bloom's Taxonomy to Develop Higher-Order Thinking

Benjamin Bloom developed a classification of intellectual behaviors important in learning ranging from the simple recall of facts (knowledge level) to more complex abstract thinking (evaluation level). Teachers tend to ask questions from their students' current knowledge level 80% to 90% of the time. To foster the critical thinking development of your students, incorporate higher-order questioning strategies into your instruction. The six levels of the taxonomy are listed from the lowest level of thinking to the most complex. As you design your classroom lessons, try to incorporate strategies that foster higher-order thinking skills.

1. **Knowledge—Dates, Places, Events, Vocabulary:**

   arrange, define, duplicate, find, label, list, locate, memorize, name, order, recognize, recall, relate, repeat, reproduce, state

2. **Comprehension—Find Meaning, Interpret Facts, Infer Cause and Effect:**

   classify, describe, discuss, explain, extend, identify, indicate, locate, predict, recognize, report, restate, review, select, summarize, translate

3. **Application—Use Information in New Situations, Solve Problems:**

   apply, change, choose, construct, demonstrate, dramatize, employ, illustrate, interpret, operate, practice, produce, schedule, show, sketch, solve, teach, use

4. **Analysis—Recognize and Explain Patterns and Meaning:**

   analyze, compare, connect, contrast, criticize, differentiate, discriminate, distinguish, examine, experiment, explain, question, prioritize, separate

5. **Synthesis—Create New Ideas, Discuss "What If" Situations, Predict and Draw Conclusions:**

   adapt, assemble, collect, compose, create, design, develop, devise, formulate, imagine, improve, manage, organize, plan, prepare, propose, set up, write

6. **Evaluation—Make Recommendations, Critique Ideas, Assess Value and Make Judgments:**

   appraise, argue, assess, attach, choose, compare, convince, debate, decide, defend, estimate, evaluate, judge, predict, rate, select, support, value

SAMPLE QUESTION STEMS

Knowledge:
- o Who, what, where, why, when . . . ?
- o Which is true or false?

Comprehension:
- o Retell . . .
- o How are . . . alike? Different?
- o What was the main idea?

Application:
- o How is . . . related to . . . ?
- o What evidence can you find to support . . . ?
- o Can you explain another instance where . . . ?
- o Can you apply this experience to another situation?

Analysis:
- o How was this similar to . . . ?
- o What do you think are other possible outcomes? Solutions?
- o How is . . . similar to . . . ?
- o What was the turning point in the story?
- o What was the problem with . . . ?
- o How does . . . compare/contrast with . . . ?

Synthesis:
- o Can you design a . . . to . . . ?
- o What might happen if . . . ?
- o Can you create a new use for . . . ?
- o What is a possible solution to . . . ?

Evaluation:
- o Is there a better solution to . . . ?
- o Defend your position about . . .
- o How would you have handled . . . ?
- o How effective are . . . ?
- o What changes to . . . would you recommend? Why?
- o What criteria would you use to assess . . . ?

SAMPLE PROJECTS AND ACTIVITIES

Knowledge:
- o Retell the story in order of events.
- o Make a facts chart.
- o List the main characters in the story.
- o List the 50 states and capitals.
- o Create a timeline of events.

Comprehension:
- o Retell the story in your own words.
- o Write a summary of the event.
- o Explain the main idea.

Application:

- o Compose a book about . . .
- o Make a game using the ideas from . . .
- o Design a market strategy for your product.
- o Make a clay model of . . .

Analysis:

- o Design a questionnaire to gather information.
- o Write a commercial for a new product.
- o Write a biography about a person being studied.
- o Review a product, book, or game.

Synthesis:

- o Create a new product.
- o Write a play about . . .
- o Create a way to . . .
- o Compose a song for . . .

Evaluation:

- o Develop a rubric for a class project.
- o Prepare a list of criteria to judge . . .
- o Participate in a debate.
- o Present your views about . . .

RESOURCE 5.3

Teacher-Selected Read Alouds,
Kindergarten Through Fifth Grade

This is a short collection of tried and true classroom favorites! The list includes both beloved classics as well as fresh new titles guaranteed to become treasured favorites.

Kindergarten and First Grade	
The Best Story	E. Spinelli
Big Words for Little People	J. L. Curtis & L. Cornell
Bootsie Barker Bites	B. Bottner
Chrysanthemum	K. Henkes
Don't Let the Pigeon Drive the Bus	M. Willams
Elephant & Piggie (series)	M. Willams
Fancy Nancy (series)	J. O'Connor
Froggy (series)	J. London
The Gruffelo	A. Scheffler
Harold and the Purple Crayon	J. Crockett
Knuffle Bunny	M. Willams
Lilly's Purple Plastic Purse	K. Henkes
No, David!	D. Shannon
Officer Buckle and Gloria	P. Rathman
Oliver Button Is a Sissy	T. dePaola
One	K. Otoshi
Owl Moon	J. Yolen
The Rainbow Fish	M. Pfister
Short Cut	D. Crew
Stella Luna	J. Cannon
Wild About Books	J. Sierra
Second and Third Grade	
The Art Lesson	T. dePaola
A Bad Case of Stripes	D. Shannon
Courage	B. Waber
The Cricket in Time Square	G. Selden
Fly Away Home	E. Bunting
Frindle	A. Clements
The Giving Tree	S. Silverstein
The Gold Coin	A. Flor Ada
Grandfather's Dance	P. MacLachlan

The Invention of Hugo Cabret	B. Selznick
James and the Giant Peach	R. Dahl
Love That Dog	S. Creech
The Meanest Thing to Say	B. Cosby
The Memory Box	M. Bahr
Miss Rumphius	B. Cooney
Mr. Lincoln's Way	P. Polacco
The Quiltmaker's Gift	J. Brumbeau
The Quiltmaker's Journey	J. Brumbeau
The Relatives Came	C. Rylant
Ruby's Wish	S. Yim
School Mouse	D. King-Smith
Stories Julian Tells	A. Cameron
The Stray	D. King-Smith
Tar Beach	F. Ringgold
Thank You, Mr. Falker	P. Palacco
The Trumpet of the Swan	E.B. White
The Wall: Growing Up Behind the Iron Curtain	P. Sis
Wilfrid Gordon McDonald Partridge	M. Fox
Zen Shorts	J. Moth
Zen Ties	J. Moth
Fourth and Fifth Grade	
An Angel for Solomon Singer	C. Rylant
Because of Winn Dixie	K. DiCamillo
Bud, Not Buddy	C. Curtis
The Cay	T. Taylor
Eggs	J. Spinelli
Good Dog	Avi
Hatchet	G. Paulsen
Holes	L. Sachar
Hoot	C. Hiaasen
The Incredible Journey of Edward Tulane	K. DiCamillo
The Jacket	A. Clement
The Kite Fighters	L. Park
Loose	J. Spinelli
The Phantom Tollbooth	N. Juster
The Series of Unfortunate Events	L. Snicket
So B. It	S. Weeks
The Tale of Despereaux	K. DiCamillo
Tuck Everlasting	N. Babbitt
Walk Two Moons	S. Creech
A Wrinkle in Time	M. L'Engle

RESOURCE 5.4

Assessment of Classroom Time on Task

Because time on task is one of the most important variables in student learning, it is vital to analyze off-task time in your classroom. The observation form in this resource will help sensitize you to time spent on organizing and on classroom interruptions that could perhaps be better spent on engaged learning time for students. Ask your aide, mentor, colleague, administrator, or student teacher to complete the time record for you during the first hour of a typical day. Analyze and discuss your data with your mentor.

OBSERVATION FORM 1

Time Spent on Organizing and on Classroom Interruptions

Teacher Name: _____ Date: _____

School: _____ Observer: _____

Observation of Classroom Time Spent on Organizing	*Time Started*	*Time Stopped*
Taking attendance		
Collecting lunch money		
Collecting homework or seat work		
Making assignments for seat work		
Making assignments for homework		
Distributing books and materials		
Explaining activities and procedures		
Organizing groups		
Shifting from one activity to another		
Disciplining students		
Observation of Classroom Interruptions	*Time Started*	*Time Stopped*
Students enter late		
Students leave early		
Parents enter		
Administrator enters		
Other visitors enter		
Loudspeaker announcements		
Special sales		
School events		
Outside noise		

RESOURCE 5.5

Effectiveness Survey: Managing Use of Classroom Time

For each practice below, circle the number of the response that most accurately describes the situation in your classroom. (5 indicates strong use; 1 indicates weak use.)

Classroom Routines and Procedures					
Class starts quickly and purposefully.	1	2	3	4	5
Materials and activities are ready when students arrive.	1	2	3	4	5
Seating is arranged to facilitate instruction.	1	2	3	4	5
Students bring needed materials to class each day.	1	2	3	4	5
Students have and use assigned storage space.	1	2	3	4	5
Administrative matters are handled routinely and efficiently.	1	2	3	4	5
Interruptions are kept to a minimum.	1	2	3	4	5
In Controlling Use of Time in My Classroom, I					
Allocate sufficient time for each subject to be taught.	1	2	3	4	5
Keep students engaged in learning for most (80 percent) of the available classroom time each day.	1	2	3	4	5
Minimize use of time for nonlearning activities.	1	2	3	4	5
Use clear start and stop cues to direct student activity.	1	2	3	4	5
Encourage students to use the clock for self-pacing.	1	2	3	4	5
Introduce new objectives and activities as quickly as possible.	1	2	3	4	5
Maintain a brisk instructional pace.	1	2	3	4	5
Require students to complete unfinished class work after school, during recess or lunch, or in other available time.	1	2	3	4	5
Use of Time in Our School Building Is Controlled So That					
The school calendar maximizes the time available for instruction.	1	2	3	4	5
New programs are evaluated relative to their impact on learning time.	1	2	3	4	5
School, classes, and other activities start and end on time.	1	2	3	4	5
The school day is organized to minimize time spent on noninstructional time.	1	2	3	4	5
Class instruction is not interrupted for routine announcements or messages.	1	2	3	4	5
Students do not have unassigned "free" time during the academic day.	1	2	3	4	5
Student pullouts during academic class time are minimized.	1	2	3	4	5

RESOURCE 5.6

Unit Construction Checklist

A curriculum unit is normally at least six or more integrated lessons. Each lesson should include two or more learning activities.

The following steps are essential to planning any unit of instruction. Indicate that you have taken each step by placing the date of satisfactory accomplishment in the blank to the left.

_____ 1. Examine your course of study to determine if/how this unit would fit into the total learning sequence.

_____ 2. Draft your instructional objectives for the teaching unit. (Three to five objectives are suggested.)

_____ 3. Clarify your expectations of pupil progress, and plan assessment activities to use with this unit.

_____ 4. In your lesson plan book, lay out a "days and topics" schedule for the unit to ensure that no principal part of the proposed coverage will be omitted from the unit.

_____ 5. Find ideas for your unit in professional books and magazines, textbooks, websites, or related commercial units.

_____ 6. Locate books and materials that may be used in the teaching of your unit.

_____ 7. Locate DVDs, websites, videos, and webcasts. Select and schedule titles of audiovisuals that seem appropriate.

_____ 9. Collect and organize materials such as pictures, displays, and models.

_____ 10. Using your "days and topics" schedule, develop at least six lesson plans to be used in this unit. (Suggestion: one lesson plan per day.)

_____ 11. Make a check mark in the blank to the left of each of the following activities that you have included in your plans:

_____ Field trip

_____ Visit by resource person

_____ Whole-class direct instruction

_____ Class discussion

_____ Small-group activities

_____ Listening to tapes

_____ Making models

_____ Making charts, diagrams, posters, maps, and graphs

_____ Making oral reports or telling stories

_____ Dramatizations/simulations

_____ Playing instructional games

_____ Making bulletin boards

_____ Making displays

_____ Integrated computer-based activities

_____ Viewing educational TV

_____ Viewing films, DVDs, or videos

_____ Viewing slides

_____ Library research

_____ Panel discussion

_____ Demonstrations

_____ Songs and/or finger plays

_____ Other:_____

_____ Other:_____

RESOURCE 5.7

Unit Planning Form

I. Duration

Dates and times: _____

II. Students

Grade level: _____

Student characteristics that need to be considered in teaching this unit: _____

_____

_____

III. Unit Topic or Theme

_____

_____

IV. Subjects

_____

_____

V. Unit Objectives

_____

_____

_____

_____

VI. Materials and Media

List curriculum books, materials, and resources to be used. Include at least one children's literature book.

_____

_____

_____

_____

VII. Procedures/Instructional Activities

A. Introduction

Procedure for introducing the unit: _____

_____

_____

_____

_____

B. Content and Activities Within the Unit

List at least six lesson topics, with preliminary notes on content, teaching strategies, activities, and assignments for each.

_____

_____

_____

_____

_____

_____

_____

C. Culminating Activity

_____

_____

_____

_____

_____

_____

VIII. Evaluation

Procedures for assessment of learner understanding: _____

_____

_____

_____

_____

_____

_____

6

Instructional Methodologies

Student Groupings, Instructional Approaches, and Instructional Strategies

A COMPREHENSIVE APPROACH TO EFFECTIVE INSTRUCTION

As you plan lessons, you will need to determine which teaching methods will be the most effective. The student groupings, instructional approaches, and instructional strategies you choose are as important to student learning as the content of the lessons you develop. In many classrooms, especially in the upper grades, teachers rely on a whole-group, teacher-centered, direct-instruction model for presenting lessons. Formal presentations by teachers compose up to one fourth of all classroom time in many schools. While this model of instruction may work well for older students, it may not be the best choice when working with elementary students. Younger learners respond to a more flexible and varied model of instruction. In general, elementary students should experience

- A succession of grouping models—whole-group, small-group, and one-to-one individualized instruction;
- A balance between a teacher-centered and student-centered approach to learning, and;
- A wide array of instructional strategies, including direct instruction, cooperative and collaborative learning, constructivist-based discovery learning, and peer learning.

While choosing the most effective model of instruction initially may seem to be a daunting task, take comfort in knowing that your expertise will develop over time. As you create your lesson plans, you will find that the content as well as the specific learning activities you select will guide these decisions.

STUDENT GROUPING

Whole-Group Presentations

Description

In the whole-group approach, a teacher or instructor tells, presents, explains, or lectures to a whole class. When using this approach, you should always use some form of visual aid. This can include a Big Book, poster, whiteboard, student samples, overhead projector, Elmo or AVerVision, or LCD projector or Smartboard. Regardless of the medium selected and the technology used for projection, it is important that you present information both visually and auditorally. All students, especially younger learners, process information more effectively when in is presented through multiple modalities, and this helps them to become more engaged in learning.

Advantages

- Presentations can serve an entire class of students at one time and in one location as they proceed together through the lesson.
- Classroom management can be easier because the whole group or class hears the presentation at one time from an instructor in a visible authority position.

Disadvantages

- Students are required to listen and remain passive learners.
- It is assumed that all students are learning the same amount of content at the same time.
- The teacher has to be enthusiastic, knowledgeable, and interesting; a lecture is a performance.
- Not all students learn at the pace set by the teacher.
- Not all students learn by listening.

How to Use Whole-Group Presentations Effectively

- Consider your purpose and rationale for presenting material in this manner—have a specific goal.
- Outline the beginning, middle, and end of the presentation. Let students know in advance how long the presentation will be.
- Decide how you will make the presentation interesting and motivating. Be sure to use a visual aid throughout your presentation.
- Remember that effective elementary teachers do not deliver long lectures with little teacher-student interaction.

- If students become fidgety, stop for a few moments, and have them stand up or get a drink of water. Guide them in a few stretching exercises before resuming your lesson. Younger students have difficulty remaining engaged for long periods during passive lessons. Offering them a chance to expel excess energy will greatly contribute to their ability to focus and remain engaged.

Quick Teaching Tips That Foster Student Involvement in Whole-Group Instruction

Ensure participation by all students in whole-group instruction by using the following strategies:

1. Call on students in a random or unpredictable pattern. Ask questions of the class in a fashion that implies that any one of them could be asked to respond. Ask the question *first,* give adequate think time, and then name the student who will answer the question.

2. When asking questions, use the "think, pair, share" strategy to encourage process time and increased participation. Pose a question, give students a few minutes to mentally formulate a response, have students discuss their ideas with a partner, and finally, randomly ask a few partners to share their collaborative responses. Using this strategy engages *all* students and not just those always eager to respond. Students are also required to think through responses and clearly articulate them to a peer before presenting them to the class.

3. Signal the class that someone else may be called on to add to, clarify, or summarize another student's response. Do *not* repeat students' answers. Require students to hear, build on, and elaborate each other's answers.

4. Make use of wait time after asking the question and after the student's initial response. Allow all students sufficient response time. Your lower-achieving students need as much time, if not more, to respond to a question than other students. If the student hesitates, waiting for him to think through an answer indicates that you feel confident that a worthwhile response is being formulated.

5. Get the students moving and doing—ask several students at a time to demonstrate a task at the whiteboard, overhead projector, or Smartboard; require seated students to perform the same task on paper or on individual whiteboards. Rotate volunteers.

6. Increase teacher-student academic interactions. Ask students more open-ended questions that require critical and creative thinking. Refer to Resource 5.2 on Bloom's Taxonomy. When you ask students to give an opinion or make a judgment about a person, situation, or idea, have them cite evidence that supports their judgment so that it is not merely a haphazard guess or recall of something you said.

7. To keep students motivated, vary your routines and materials. Provide frequent shifts of activities as opposed to expecting students to just listen for long periods. Limit your lessons to 10 minutes or fewer. It is better to present lessons in a series of mini-lessons than one long lesson.

8. Make certain that high, yet reasonable expectations for all students are clearly stated and modeled. Provide equitable response opportunities by calling on *all* the children, not just those with their hands up or those you think will have a correct or thoughtful response.

Small Groups

Description

Small group instruction is when students work together in groups of three to six. It is well recognized that younger or emergent learners learn better in smaller-size groups. Membership to a specific instructional group is temporary and is contingent on the purpose of the group. Peer interaction is encouraged in small groups to foster social and communication skills as well as academic understanding. Some formations of small groups include the following:

- Interest groups (students self-select membership based on a desire to study a particular book or concept)
- Instructional groups (teacher selects a group of students who demonstrate a similar academic need, learning style, or level of ability in a specific skill)
- Cooperative or collaborative groups (students work collaboratively toward a common goal)
- Pairs (two students work together to achieve a common goal)

Advantages

- Social and communication skills are enhanced as students work with each other.
- Teachers can obtain immediate feedback, learning more about the effectiveness of a lesson by listening to students' discussions.
- Active learning and higher-level thinking are promoted.
- Individual students have the opportunity to share ideas, solve problems, support, and scaffold each other's learning, and discuss materials with their peers.

Disadvantages and Challenges

- Small-group instruction is not as efficient as whole-group instruction.
- Careful consideration must be given to group formation, composition, and learning objectives.
- For younger students, small-group work is most effective when the teacher facilitates or leads the group. This can lead to management challenges for the remainder of the class.
- Routines and procedures for students not participating in the small group must be clearly defined, understood, and practiced.

- If the teacher is facilitating or leading the small group, meaningful activities must be provided for the remainder of the class. Avoid assigning busywork to keep the remainder of the class occupied.

When to Use Small Groups

- Use small groups to foster peer discussion and interaction. Students can discuss topics and exchange facts, ideas, and opinions. Students may offer different viewpoints or personal experiences. Groups can solve open-ended problems, read case studies, and engage in role-playing and simulation. Educational games can be used to facilitate learning.
- Small-group work is effective when using hands-on materials or manipulatives.
- Use small groups when building or constructing projects.

One-to-One Instruction

Description

During one-to-one (1:1) instruction, a student works individually with a teacher, a paraprofessional (which would include a student teacher or instructional aide), a learning specialist, or a parent volunteer. One-to-one instruction can be accommodated within the classroom setting ("push-in") or outside the classroom ("pull-out").

Advantages

- Instruction can be targeted to the student's individual needs or learning style.
- Feedback is immediate for both teacher and student.
- The teacher can assess student performance during instruction.

Disadvantages and Challenges

- This style of instruction is time intensive.
- It presents classroom management challenges.
- Other students may vie for teacher attention.
- Students pulled out of the regular classroom for 1:1 support may feel isolated or "different" from their peers.

Individualized Learning

Description

Individualized learning is also known as self-paced learning. Unlike whole-group presentations, its structure requires active, individualized participation by each student. The teacher provides objectives and direction for the student, along with a carefully designed set of learning activities to be completed in small, sequential steps.

Advantages

- Students work according to their personal abilities. Learners at risk, as well as gifted students, complete the instruction on their own time schedule.

- The teacher can work more easily with an individual student and tailor instruction to meet individual needs.
- Students' effective study habits are reinforced and rewarded.

Disadvantages

- Additional time may be needed to teach and reinforce students' self-regulation in order for them to keep progressing.
- Additional work is required of the teacher to prepare and grade personalized student learning materials and activities.
- Lack of variety in self-paced materials can be monotonous.
- The teacher and student may not interact much in a self-paced program.
- Feedback is limited and difficult to give in a timely fashion. Misconceptions, errors, and lack of requisite knowledge may go undetected.

How to Use Self-Paced Learning Effectively

- Provide enrichment to students who wish to learn more about a given subject.
- Give individual students needed additional practice in a given subject.
- Allow students to practice rote facts or skills at their own pace.

Sample Types of Self-Paced Learning Materials

- Self-instructional packages (SIPs): Designed to teach a relatively small amount of materials to the mastery level, an SIP is a learning packet developed for an individual student using small, sequential steps and giving frequent, immediate feedback to the learner.
- Tutorial CDs and worksheets: The instructor's voice on the CD tells the student what to read or what problem to solve. The recording gives directions and explanations of answers.
- Computer-based instruction: Often used as a drill-and-practice activity, computer-based instruction gives an individual student immediate feedback. Some programs adapt instruction on the basis of the learner's performance.
- Individualized inquiry investigations: The student presents to the teacher an issue, topic, or problem in which the student has personal interest. A contract is drawn up to specify the conditions of the investigation, for example, how much time should be devoted to it, whether the student should be excused from class to pursue the investigation, how the student will report results, and how the investigation will be evaluated.

INSTRUCTIONAL APPROACHES

Deciding on which instructional approach you will use is as important as deciding the goals and objectives of your lesson. Generally speaking, your instructional approach sets the tone for the entire learning experience. A teacher-centered approach is used when you want to deliver specific information to students. A student-centered approach is used when you want to act more as a guide or facilitator. The goals and objectives of the lessons you create will guide your instructional approach.

Teacher-Centered Approach

Description

A teacher-centered approach to learning and instruction has a long history in education. This approach is modeled after the "master and apprentice" approach to learning. In a teacher-centered lesson, the teacher is viewed as the expert. The goal is to impart specific and accurate knowledge or a set of skills to the students. In a teacher-centered lesson:

- The focus is on the teacher;
- The teacher does most of the talking, and students listen;
- Students primarily work alone, and the classroom is quiet;
- The teacher answers student questions about learning;
- The teacher chooses topics and the direction of the lessons; and
- The teacher is responsible for assessing student learning.

Advantages

- The teacher can direct learning and plan how lessons should proceed.
- The teacher knows what has been taught and what needs to be taught.
- The teacher can maintain control of student behavior.
- The teacher presents material accurately, systematically, and comprehensively. Gaps in student knowledge and misconceptions are avoided.

Disadvantages

- Learning is passive.
- Students may demonstrate a lack of motivation or interest.
- Students may have difficulty seeing the "relevance" of the lesson.
- Learning is independent and contingent upon the individual's ability to process the information in the way it is presented.

When to Use a Teacher-Centered Approach

A teacher-centered approach may be the best choice when teaching foundational skills. The goal in skill instruction is for students to obtain mastery of a skill set and to be able to transfer or use these skills in more project-based or content-based learning activities. Teacher-centered instruction is also a useful approach for teaching the background knowledge necessary for future learning activities. When using a teacher-centered approach, regardless of whether you are teaching a large or small group, refer to the tips for effective whole-group instruction presented earlier in this chapter.

Student-Centered Approach

Description

In a student-centered approach to instruction, the teacher assumes the role as guide, facilitator, or resource in student learning. Students are expected to actively engage in their learning through discussion, questioning, debating, brainstorming, planning, and reflection. In a student-centered lesson:

- The focus is on both the teacher and the student;
- The teacher models expectations, and students are expected to actively take responsibility for their learning;
- Student groupings are flexible; students work in pairs, small groups, and individually, depending on lesson goals or objectives;
- Peer interaction is encouraged; students work together to answer each other's questions and solve problems, and the teacher serves as a resource;
- Students have some choice on topics, activities, and projects;
- Self-assessment is encouraged, as students and the teacher evaluate student learning; and
- The classroom is busy, noisy, and active.

Advantages of the Student-Centered Approach

The student-centered approach

- Is associated with increases in student motivation.
- Is associated with an increased use of self-regulated learning skills, such as self-monitoring, self-direction, and self-evaluation.
- Fosters students' independence, responsibility, accountability, and overall sense of autonomy.
- Creates an interdependence between the student and the teacher.

Disadvantages of the Student-Centered Approach

- The teacher may feel a lack of control over the content and direction of the lessons.
- Students may not have sufficient or adequate skills or background knowledge to meet the objectives of the lesson.

When to Use a Student-Centered Approach

A student-centered approach to instruction is best used when you are certain that students have mastery of the required skills or content knowledge to successfully meet the goals and objective of the lesson. This approach is especially effective for project-based learning activities, book groups, or book clubs. An important aspect of student-centered learning is student choice. Look for opportunities throughout all of your lessons, regardless of whether you are using a more teacher-centered or student-centered approach, to embed student choice.

INSTRUCTIONAL STRATEGIES

The instructional strategies you choose should be directly aligned with the needs of your students and your desired student outcomes. Having a repertoire of effective strategies keeps students engaged and keeps the learning more interesting and vibrant. Skill-based lessons are a major part of the elementary curriculum. The repetitive practice necessary to achieve fluency and mastery of specific skills can become routine, predictable, and tiresome. Using a variety of instructional strategies will keep lessons fresh and will increase student motivation. Resource 6.1 provides a comprehensive list of possible instructional strategies.

Cooperative Learning

Cooperative learning is an instructional strategy widely recognized as both effective and engaging. It is one of the most researched instructional strategies. Cooperative learning has been shown to have positive effects on academic achievement, collaborative behavior, crosscultural understandings and relationships, and attitudes toward students with disabilities. Cooperative learning is more than just students working in a small-group format. Cooperative learning requires interdependence, trust, effective communication, and a willingness to work collaboratively toward a common goal. Each student is responsible for her own learning as well as helping "teammates" learn. Cooperative efforts result in mutual benefits for all members.

Guidelines for Using Cooperative Learning

- Limit group size to three to five students.
- Compose groups heterogeneously by mixing students with regard to academic achievement, gender, social skills, and ethnicity/race.
- Give each student in the group a specific role, responsibility, or task that contributes to the success of the total group. Be careful to rotate roles and responsibilities as well as create tasks that foster interdependence.
- Use cooperative learning as a supplemental activity for review, enrichment, or practice, allowing students in the group opportunities to help one another master material. Cooperative learning is also effective for student-centered, project-based activities, such as reports, presentations, and experiments.
- Consider room arrangement, task materials, and time frame as you plan cooperative activities.
- Assess and grade individual students' contributions as well as the whole group's products and presentations.
- Consider evaluating and grading groups on affective, less tangible aspects of learning, such as quality of discussions, willingness to work together, and positive and supportive social interactions.
- Vary group composition so that no student feels labeled by being in a "slow" group and so all students have an opportunity during the school year to work with every other student in the class.
- For cooperative learning groups to function effectively, collaborative social skills must be taught, modeled, and reinforced regularly.

Direct Instruction

Direct instruction is another widely researched instructional strategy. In contrast to cooperative learning, which encompasses a student-centered approach, direct instruction is more closely aligned with a teacher-centered approach to instruction. The direct instruction model includes six specific steps:

1. Gain students' attention
2. Review past learning
3. Present new information (demonstrate or model)
4. Assist students in performing the tasks (guided practice)
5. Provide independent practice
6. Review lesson

During the first step, you should explicitly state the goal or objective of the lesson. Independent practice should be delayed until you are certain that students will be able to perform the skill with a 90% accuracy rate.

Learning Centers

Learning centers or stations are a way to individualize and personalize learning. A learning center is a place to which children can go to do an instructional task on their own (or with a partner), completing the activity outlined there. Following are some important considerations when designing learning centers:

- Make sure written directions and all the materials needed to complete the task are available at the station.
- Consider leaving an answer key or correcting guide in the center to enable students who finish the task to self-correct.
- Centers are usually set up in classroom corners or along walls so that children face a bulletin board. Sometimes, you can place bookshelves or file cabinets perpendicular to the wall to create a specific center area.

Computer Technology and Instruction

Computer use in education is categorized into two levels: low-level technology and high-level technology. Low-level technology tends to be associated with teacher-centered practices, and high-level technology tends to be associated with student-centered practices. In general, teachers predominately use technology for transmitting information rather than as a tool to help learners actively construct knowledge. Students' use of technology is frequently limited to computer-based activities that include creating products, expressing themselves in writing, improving computer skills, doing research on the Internet, and doing practice drills. While technology can be very effective for creating, presenting, and sharing information, it can also be used as an invaluable tool to enhance learning and instruction.

The 21st century is characterized as a technology and media-suffused environment marked by rapid changes in technology tools, immediate access to an abundance of information, and the ability to communicate across the globe. It has recently been acknowledged that in order to be effective in the 21st century, students, citizens, and workers must be able to exhibit a range of functional and critical thinking skills related to information, media, and technology. The 21st-century teacher must create authentic and relevant learning environments that enable students to master the knowledge, skills, and expertise to succeed in school, work, and life. Instructional practices characterized as high-level uses of technology play an integral role in this challenge. The importance of effective uses of technology in education is recognized at both the national and international level. The Partnership for 21st Century Skills (P21) is a national organization that advocates for the integration of skills such as critical thinking, problem solving, and communication into core academic subjects. Toward this end, P21 has developed 21st-century student outcomes for technology.

The International Society for Technology in Education (ISTE) has also focused on the effective integration of technology in education. The organization has developed National Educational Technology Standards (NETS) for students and teachers. The goal of the NETS is for students and teachers to learn to use technology as a communication tool, a problem-solving tool, and as a research tool.

As a new teacher, it is important not to regard technology as just one more thing to teach to your students. Technology should be seen as a tool for learning. Students do not learn "technology"; rather, they use technology to support their learning. Think of the many ways in which technology has enhanced your own life. Do you communicate with family and friends through social networks? Texting? E-mail? Did you use technology throughout your teacher credential program for research? Distance learning? Networking with classmates? As you develop your craft, you will continually find new and better ways to enhance both your teaching and learning with the use of technology. Both the Partnership for 21st Century Learning as well as the International Society for Technology in Education have wonderful websites to support you in your journey:

Partnership for 21st Century Learning: http://www.21stcenturyskills.org

International Society for Technology in Education: http://cnets.iste.org/students/s_stands.html

Technology and Reading Fluency

With the use of classroom computers, laptops, and handheld devices such as an iTouch, iPad, and other common recording applications, students can easily learn to record themselves independently reading a selected passage or text. Using this technology, students can play back recordings and self-evaluate their ability to read with expression and fluency. This metacognitive process supports students' use of self-regulating strategies (e.g., goal setting, self-monitoring, and self-evaluation). Student recordings can easily be played back for the student to hear and can be shared with parents through e-mail. Recordings can also be saved to create an artifact for a portfolio. Students and teachers can compare early recordings to later ones to assess fluency development over time. Technology used in this way becomes a tool to enhance student learning.

Learning Through the Use of Manipulatives

All elementary teachers understand the value of manipulatives as an important learning tool for younger students. Manipulatives provide a tangible and concrete way for students to visualize abstract concepts or processes. As a new teacher, you may find that your classroom does not come equipped with all the manipulatives you have seen in veteran teacher's classrooms. The truth is that this collection of resources and learning tools takes times to build. Fortunately, the National Library of Virtual Manipulatives is an excellent resource for any new teachers who may not have the time or resources to stock their classroom with a vast array of learning tools.

National Library of Virtual Manipulatives: http://nlvm.usu.edu/en/nav/vlibrary.html

Using Technology to Modify Text for Students With Special Needs

Using technology as a tool to assist and accommodate students with special needs is critical. Modifications to classroom lessons and materials are quite easy to implement and can greatly enhance learning. Changing screen color, enlarging font, highlighting onscreen text, and increasing spacing between words are simple modifications teachers and students can make for learning to be more accessible. Worksheets and other text can be modified in a similar fashion. Scanning worksheets as PDFs and having them read aloud can be accomplished by using Adobe Acrobat Standard.

Hypermedia and Electronic Texts

The use of hypertext (highlighted text that links to underlying definitions or supporting or related text, almost like an electronic footnote) offers an instructional advantage to many students. Following are descriptions of only a few of the many electronic books and hypermedia systems that exemplify how technology impacts the ways lessons are taught and applied in many elementary classrooms.

Schools across the country use simple hypertext systems such as the CD-ROM based on *Compton's Illustrated Encyclopedia* or the *Grolier Electronic Encyclopedia*. In the case of the *Grolier Electronic Encyclopedia*, 21 volumes, 33 thousand articles, and nine million words of text are available. By typing in a single search word (e.g., *whales*), the student can make the system search every reference to the subject in the encyclopedia. An electronic cutting and editing system allows the student to take notes and compile a personalized data bank.

Another example of hypertext or *hypermedia* (hypertext and visual and auditory sources) is the Smart Books program by Scholastic. In this program, electronic books based on existing traditional print books are rendered electronically to take advantage of CD-ROM and hypermedia technologies. As an example, the Smart Book version of *If Your Name Was Changed at Ellis Island*, by Ellen Levine, lets children hear stories of immigrants' trips through Ellis Island, meet famous Ellis Island immigrants, meet contemporary immigrant children, use maps and graphs, explore the Ellis Island complex, and visit a Japanese-American internment camp.

Another example, *M-ss-ng L-nks*, is an old favorite of reading teachers that is now available in a new format. Students of all ability levels can engage in language play with this award-winning material from Sunburst Communications. In *M-ss-ng L-nks*, passages from well-known children's books, as well as from science and encyclopedic materials, appear as engaging word puzzles. Each passage is presented in cloze format. Students fill in the blanks based on their knowledge of language structure, spelling patterns, context clues, and literary style. Students can work individually, in pairs, or in a collaborative group to solve each puzzle. As they make correct choices, a picture related to the passage can be revealed. Reports can be printed to summarize student responses.

Fostering Communication Beyond the Classroom Walls

The Internet provides an easy way for students to communicate with others outside their immediate school environment. One teacher, for example, arranged for her second graders to regularly correspond with a fellow teacher who had taken a year off to bicycle around the world. Through their online discussions using Skype, iChat, and e-mail, the students learned about world languages, cultures, geography, art, time zones, and architecture while improving their skills in reading, writing, and communicating. Other teachers have set up pen pal relationships with students in different regions of the country or the world, enabling children to learn from each other about all kinds of global issues while simultaneously improving their communication skills and respect for diversity.

Other teachers have developed buddy projects between classes studying similar subjects. One class doing a field study of pond life at a local site compared notes with children doing a similar study at a pond in another region. In another innovative program, a first-grade class created a "butterfly garden." A sixth-grade class in the same district partnered with them to develop a website to document their project.

Using the Internet as a Resource

In addition to being a tool used to enhance instruction and learning, the Internet also contains many wonderful resources available to teachers who want supplementary information to expand their expertise on a given topic. Lesson plans and informational resources for students are also widely available.

Websites for Lesson Plans and Ideas

- Super Teacher Worksheets: http://www.superteacherworksheets .com/syllables.html

- The Educator's Reference Desk: http://ericir.syr.edu/Virtual/Lessons/
- TEAMS Educational Resources: http://teams.lacoe.edu/
- Scholastic's Teacher Resources: http://teacher.scholastic.com/index.htm
- Smithsonian Education: http://www.smithsonianeducation.org/educators/
- Kathy Schrock's Guide for Educators: http://discoveryschool.com/schrockguide/index.html
- Thinkfinity—Thousands of Standards-Based Lesson Plans for Teachers: http://www.thinkfinity.org/lesson-plans
- Time for Kids: Teachers: http://www.timeforkids.com/TFK/

Websites for Classroom Literature,
Book Reviews, and Related Activities

- American Library Association: http://www.ala.org/alsc
- Carol Hurst Children's Literature Site: http://www.carolhurst.com
- Children's Literature Web Guide: http://www.acs.ucalgary.ca/~dkbrown
- Multicultural Book Reviews: http://www.isomedia.com/homes/jmele/joe.html
- Multicultural Calendar: http://www.kidlink.org/KIDPROJ/MCC

For a list of Internet sites by content domain, refer to Resource 6.2. Remember, a good site may lead you to other good sites through related links. Share your finds with colleagues; sharing is one of the best ways to discover new resources!

Bringing It All Together

As you create your individual lesson plans and curriculum units, be sure to consider the effectiveness of your overall teaching methodology. This includes instructional grouping choices, your instructional approach, and the instructional strategies you plan to use. Designing your lessons from this broader perspective will greatly enhance the quality and effectiveness of your teaching. Use the questions below as a guide while you plan and reflect on your lessons.

1. Did I select the best form of grouping for this particular activity? How would a small-group approach change the lesson? Whole group?

2. Does the content of this particular lesson require a teacher-centered approach or could I utilize a more student-centered approach?

3. When using a teacher-centered approach, how and where can I offer student choice?

4. Have I selected the best instructional strategy for this particular lesson?

5. Have I varied my instructional strategies to keep lessons fresh and engaging?

6. How can I incorporate technology as a student learning tool?

STUDENT DIVERSITY

Effective Instruction for All Students

As a new teacher, you will be faced with the challenge of working with a diverse student population. Regardless of where you work, the students you teach will bring with them a range of learning styles, languages, abilities, and different background experiences. Understanding, appreciating, respecting student diversity, and developing effective strategies to enhance individual learning are continual goals for all educators.

Students at Risk

Teachers continually struggle with getting through tremendous amounts of curriculum while ensuring that students are learning and demonstrating proficiency in what they are expected to know at each grade level. Differentiating instruction to meet the needs of each student is an ideal goal but one that is constantly challenging. How do you adapt your instruction to meet the needs of students who may be demonstrating work that is below grade-level benchmarks and may even be at risk of failing in your classroom?

"At-risk for school failure" is a term that refers to factors that are associated with lower measures of academic achievement. Children living in single-parent families, in families receiving welfare assistance, in families having a non-English primary language in the home, and children whose mothers have less than a high school education, are particularly at risk.

There are many things you, as a teacher, cannot change to reduce the child's risk factors. But, it is important that you do what you can to help the student at risk in the classroom. Because of this, intervention is critical during the early years. Children who start behind in school usually stay behind. Without additional attention to children who are struggling in your classroom, the student who is at risk will most likely fall behind and stay behind, ever widening their achievement gap.

Contrary to what you might expect, there is little need for qualitatively different forms of instruction for students who differ in aptitude and achievement level. Providing additional structure and support, while retaining the best and effective teaching strategies that work with *all* students, is crucial. Be careful not to have lowered expectations for students at risk. Emphasize higher-level thinking, problem solving, new challenges, and the excitement of learning. Even though students who may be at risk may need more instructional time and practice, they may experience apathy and boredom from low-level worksheets, which they may find tedious and trivial. For these children especially, school should be a place that is challenging, fun, and interesting.

Each of the strategies listed below is characteristic of good instruction in general. For your students at risk, in particular, teaching in this manner is crucial.

EFFECTIVE INSTRUCTION FOR STUDENTS AT RISK

Characteristic	Description
Greater structure and support	Class expectations need to be laid out clearly, and assignments and assessments need to be designed to encourage achievement and the feeling of success.
Active teaching	The teacher needs to deliver the content to students personally through interactive teaching rather than depending on curricular materials, such as the text or workbooks, particularly for children for whom English is their second language.
Instruction emphasizing student engagement	Interactive teaching with high-questioning levels invites all students to participate in lessons. Activity-based teaching/learning, small-group instruction, and/or individualized instruction are used. Practice is frequent, and instruction uses different modalities to engage students and address all learning styles.
More-frequent feedback	Student progress should be monitored frequently through classroom questions and assignments. The teacher regularly discusses progress and growth with students.
Smaller steps with more redundancy	Content should be broken down into smaller steps, and student mastery should be ensured before moving on to the next step. Constant review of earlier materials provides for overlearning. Scaffolding should be paced according to individual student progress.
Higher success rates	Classroom questions, assignments, and assessments should be designed to maximize opportunities for success, feelings of independence, self-confidence, and a heightened sense of self-esteem that comes from the joy of learning and thrill of success.

Suggestions for Helping Students With Special Learning Needs

Many times, elementary students struggling in school are reluctant to fully participate in classroom activities. Risking participation carries with it the possibility of more failure. You must find ways to create a welcome and accepting classroom environment in which students feel safe to take risks and participate without the fear of failure.

You will find that many of the children in your class experience different learning challenges and needs. For those children who already have Individual Education Plans (IEPs), some support from resource staff is most likely implemented during the student's instructional hours. But, many children who are not categorized as "Special Ed" experience difficulty in the classroom in different ways. For some, reading proficiency comes late and has been difficult. For children who read below grade level, writing can be especially challenging. Many children struggle with learning abstract concepts in math. Some children have a difficult time getting started on a writing project, or they may have difficulty focusing on and attending to a task. Behavior and/or emotional problems often accompany learning problems. You will find that for many children, school can be stressful and create anxiety because of fear of failure. Find out what your school policies are for identifying students who you think may be in need of further support and intervention. Don't let them slip between the cracks, and make sure they are on the radar of your entire teaching staff. Give students frequent and positive feedback, and provide them with significant successful experiences. In general, whatever strategies you use to increase the effectiveness of your overall classroom instruction will have disproportionately high positive effects on your underachieving students.

Encouraging respect for all classmates provides a foundation in which all students feel supported, welcome, and are not afraid to make a mistake. Adapt and modify materials, lessons, and procedures to the needs of struggling students. Break complex learning into simpler components, moving from the most concrete to the most abstract. Make provisions for your learners who learn best through tactile and kinesthetic modalities. Become familiar with your students' learning styles or preferences, and vary your lessons, using different individual tasks and capitalizing on students' abilities. Build on strengths. What special abilities do your students who are lower achieving possess? How can you incorporate these abilities throughout the curriculum?

Having buddies, such as supported or "buddy" reading, is one way to build trust, friendship, and acceptance of all. Allow students to read aloud together, taking turns or reading in unison. Encourage art projects, Reader's Theater, and science projects in small groups of children who will support those who may otherwise struggle while working independently. Provide peer or adult tutoring whenever possible for your children with learning needs. Any volunteers you can pull into your classroom to help students who need some extra time, practice, and attention will be well worth it. Involve the student's parents, and try to collaborate with them, so the child feels supported and valued by both you and their family.

CHILDREN WITH DIVERSE BACKGROUNDS

Schools in this country, particularly public schools, are growing in their student diversity. Student populations today are composed of large numbers of children from increasingly different racial, ethnic, and cultural backgrounds. What has been considered the "traditional" family is also changing. Many children today come from single-parent homes, same-gender parents, multiethnic backgrounds, mixed families from mixed marriages, grandparents living at home and/or raising children, parents who are both working outside the home, and a myriad of background experiences that many teachers are unfamiliar with first hand. Teachers need to recognize this diversity, embrace it, respect it, and organize their classroom activities accordingly to encompass all children and all families with fairness and caring.

Ethnic and Cultural Differences

Racial and ethnic diversity has grown dramatically in the United States in the last three decades. The population is projected to become even more diverse in the decades to come. According to the Federal Interagency Forum on Child and Family Statistics (2009), 56% of children ages below the age of 17 in the United States are white, non-Hispanic; 22% are Hispanic; 15% are Black/African American; 4% are Asian; and 5% are of other races. This tremendous diversity brings a host of cultural and language differences to most classrooms across the country. As you review school records at the start of the year, learn the ethnic and cultural backgrounds of your students and the languages they speak at home. Find out what language the child's family uses at home, and whether the parents also speak English and to what extent. Learn about cultural differences and how different societies perceive the role of the teacher.

Communicate clearly to your class that you value and respect all children and that you expect the same from them toward each other. Include families in the classroom, and welcome them to share festivals, holidays, and nonreligious practices with the class and to build respect for all and a better understanding of cultural differences. The important thing is your students' understanding that we are all Americans, regardless of our backgrounds.

Student Mobility

School mobility may lead to some disruption in learning. Students who change schools frequently, referred to as "transient" in the past, often suffer from low academic achievement. Between 13% to 15% of all children between the ages of 5 to 14 moved within the United States primarily because of housing-related issues. Migrant families, who move for work-related reasons and whose children attend school intermittently, often present challenges to teachers struggling to help the child fit in and catch up. Find out as soon as possible which of your children are new to the area and may need help getting settled in your classroom, the school, and the community. As you work with these new students, be particularly aware of their needs. Be prepared to spend extra time, effort, and care. Many children experience academic difficulties, often being the cause of poor school attendance, delay of school records—which may contain important and sensitive information—being incorrectly placed in a program or classroom, and loss of social relationships and consistency. Mobile students frequently tend to experience other difficulties, too, such as low-income and single-parent households. Find ways to include newcomers into the daily routines of the classroom. Contact the new families immediately, and invite them into your classroom, so they can get to know you and the other children and families. Make sure they get as much information as they can about your classroom and plans for the school year, the school calendar and general school information, and community resources, such as the library and the parks. You may find that children entering from other cities, states, and school districts have had different academic standards. Try to assess their abilities as soon as they are comfortable so that you can give them any academic support they might need as early as possible. Do what you can to make the child and family feel happy to be in your classroom and integrated into the classroom and school environment.

Family Status

Children live in a variety of settings and with many different types of families. The structure of children's families is associated with the economic, parental, and community resources available to children. In 2008, 67% of children under the age of 17 lived with two parents (Federal Interagency Forum on Child and Family Statistics, 2009). While most children spend the majority of their childhood living with two parents, some children have other living arrangements. The information you can gather about the presence of parents and other adults in the family, including a parent's unmarried partner, grandparents, and other relatives, is critically important for understanding children's social, economic, and developmental well-being. Be sensitive and nonjudgmental about all your students' family structures. Be inclusive of all primary caregivers, such as grandparents or other adult caregivers, and make sure that they get the same level of attention, information, and communication about their child and your classroom as biological parents do.

Poverty

Compared with children living in families that are not in poverty, children living in poverty are more likely to have difficulty in school, to become teen parents, and to earn less and be unemployed more frequently as adults. In 2007, almost one in five children under the age of 18 currently lived in poverty (Federal Interagency Forum on Child and Family Statistics, 2009). In your review of school records, pay particular attention to students who are eligible for free or reduced-price lunches. They may come into school hungry; may need a snack, some warm or clean clothes, and school materials; and may need extra help overall. In addition, watch for poverty among children from single-parent homes. Children living in single-parent families are more likely to live in poverty than children living in a household with two parents (Federal Interagency Forum on Child and Family Statistics, 2009).

Teaching to Diversity

To teach the wide variety of students found in any one classroom, you will need to organize your classroom activities so that all students can participate meaningfully. The use of integrated curriculum, collaborative projects, and learning centers; the creation of multilevel curriculum units; and the recognition of multiple intelligences are all necessary responses to student diversity in the classroom. You also need to consider the climate of your whole school. How is diversity represented and celebrated throughout the school? What is on the walls? What is the content and format of school assemblies? Whose customs or holidays are represented on the bulletin boards in the hallways? If there are non-English speakers in your school, are there signs or posters in their languages? Are other languages represented even in monolingual schools? Does the school promote multiculturalism during school assemblies and throughout the year?

You might want to check out the classic resource on student diversity, the Teaching Tolerance project created by the Southern Poverty Law Center in 1991. This project provides teachers with low-cost or free resources to develop students' understanding of and respect for others. Resources described on the project's website (www.splcenter.org/what-we-do/teaching-tolerance) include posters, videos, and books, plus the free semiannual magazine *Teaching Tolerance.*

More Information on How Student Populations Are Changing

For a complete, updated picture of the demographics and schools in our country today, the site of the National Center for Education Statistics (http://nces.ed.gov) provides extensive data, including the *Encyclopedia of Educational Statistics.* For other authoritative demographic information, visit the Forum on Child and Family Statistics (www.childstats.gov); this site provides easy access to all U.S. government websites with statistics about children and families. Full-text reports on this site include *America's Children: Key National Indicators of Well-Being.*

Second-Language Learners

English language learner (ELL) services were provided to 3.8 million students during the 2003 to 2004 school year. ELL students are those whose primary language (the language spoken at home) is one other than English. The percentage of children who speak English with varying degrees of difficulty varies by region of the country. California and Texas have had the largest number of students receiving ELL services during the past several years (National Center for Education Statistics, 2009).

Children whose primary language is one other than English are usually referred to as "English-as-a-second-language" (ESL) or "limited-English-proficient" (LEP) students. ESL instruction is frequently provided in a pull-out program, in which ESL children are placed in regular classrooms for most or all of the day but attend separate classes or are given small-group English language instruction for a part of the day. Some schools offer transitional bilingual classes taught by bilingual teachers. You will most likely have children in your classroom with limited English proficiency.

Specific guidelines for working with LEP students are the subject of numerous current books, articles, professional development, and coursework. In general, the LEP recommendations are good for *all* children in your classroom, and they provide an activity-based, hands-on, interactive, engaging, and caring class environment. The following teaching methods foster English language development:

- Using the most concrete, most context-rich (least abstract) forms of instruction
- Supplementing the basal reader as much as possible with high-interest fiction and nonfiction books
- Creating a literacy-rich environment in the classroom
- Using small-group, mixed-ability, cooperative learning, and collaborative projects
- Encouraging extensive reading—read alouds, guided reading, shared reading, and independent and partner reading
- Concentrating on the use of multisensory approaches, using various learning modalities—visual, auditory, verbal, tactile, and kinesthetic
- Incorporating technology and audiovisual materials, such as videos, computer software, music, photographs, and pictures
- Modeling clear and understandable spoken English

Cultural Diversity in the Classroom

Effective beginning teachers celebrate the great diversity of cultures and ethnic heritages in their classrooms. Understanding and being sensitive to the multicultural identities of students allows teachers to serve them better. Effective teachers strive to both improve the quality of human relations in the classroom and also to promote students' appreciation for the multicultural composition of their classroom, school, community, and globally; and to help students appreciate who they are as individuals.

The percentage of full-time teachers who are racial/ethnic minorities is growing, although in 2004 it was only 17% (National Center for Education Statistics, 2009). We, as teachers, make up a much less diverse group of professionals than the students we teach. Take time in your classroom to develop awareness and appreciation for cultural diversity. You will help foster respect for the differences in *all* children and create a more empathic, accepting climate in your classroom. As professional educators, it is imperative that we all work to build positive multilingual, multiethnic, and multicultural human relations and foster equity and collaboration in our schools.

The following general suggestions may be helpful in your classroom.

- Acknowledge the importance of having pride in one's background.
- Encourage students to be supportive of friendships that cross cultural, racial, and ethnic boundaries.
- Have students discuss differences and similarities between cultures.
- Be flexible in your expectations for performance (e.g., students from other cultures may not be accustomed to speaking loudly in front of others).
- Present a curriculum that reflects, respects, and appreciates the cultural diversity of your student population. Include families and cultural interactions and activities as much as possible.

In addition, be alert to certain negative behaviors that occasionally occur between culturally diverse groups. For example, students sometimes

- Ridicule other students' use of the English language or their primary language;
- Mimic other students because of cultural differences;
- Assume that all students celebrate the same holidays; and
- Ridicule customs, dress, foods, and behaviors of different ethnic groups.

You need to adopt a zero-tolerance policy for any such negative behaviors in your classroom.

Obviously, there are many challenges in creating an excellent learning environment for every child in today's diverse classroom. Where do you start? You may need to personally make time to learn about people from cultures you have less knowledge in. Read books, articles, and magazines. You will gain a better understanding—along with new teaching ideas. Also, get to know your students. Talk with them. Talk with their families and with people in the community.

You may find the following suggestions helpful:

- If you feel a bit of anxiety about working with students whose culture is unfamiliar to you, realize such feelings are normal and will soon fade as you become more knowledgeable and comfortable.
- Be aware that cultures may differ in attitudes toward educational methods (i.e., cooperation vs. competition), schoolwork, respect for elders, learning styles, and so forth. By being aware of these potential differences, you will reduce the possibility of misunderstanding and miscommunication.
- Consider the issue of respect. For example, in some elementary schools today, teachers are addressed by their first names. In many cultures, however, this is disrespectful. Issues of respect also include etiquette for answering questions and for volunteering—is it seen as boasting, showing off, or acceptable behavior?
- Give all students an opportunity to contribute their perspectives and experiences in class. Value everyone's contributions. Your expectations for individual students affect your relationships with them in and out of class. Expect that each child will succeed.
- Think carefully about how you assign students to various learning groups in your classroom.

RESOURCE 6.1

Effective Instructional Strategies

Activating Prior Knowledge: Help learners connect to concepts about to be taught by using activities that relate to the content or determine the level of their existing knowledge about the subject.

Air Drawing: Students draw or motion in the air to demonstrate a particular skill or how they will carry out a procedure before they actually do so.

Alphabet Summary: Each student is assigned a different letter of the alphabet and asked to generate a word starting with that letter that is related to the topic being discussed.

Author's Chair: Students sit in a chair at the front of the class and present their work to the class. All other students give feedback, constructive criticism, and/or praise.

Blogs: Blogs, also known as weblogs, are online journals that can be used by the teacher as a means of sharing thoughts, assignments, or resources. Students can create or respond to blogs for the purpose of intergroup communication or as part of class assignments.

Brainstorming: This is a group process in which all ideas are accepted and recorded (usually by the teacher).

Case Studies: Students consider real-life problems that they discuss and problem solve.

Class Publication: Students collaborate to create a written work to be published. Formats might include magazine, newspaper, brochure, map, or newsletter.

Cloze Procedure: The teacher selects a passage of text, marks out some of the words, and then rewrites the text with blank lines where the marked out words were. The result is a "fill in the blank" that should be enjoyable for the students while at the same time giving the teacher information about the students' language skills.

Cross-Age Tutoring: Older students act as tutors to younger students. This is often carried out in the form of a "buddy" program.

Dialectical Journal: A dialectical journal is a two-column note-taking or journal method that features quotes or ideas from the text in one column and ideas from the reader in the other column.

Discussion Web: This is a discussion that begins with individual students formulating a response, then each student pairs with one other, and then the pairs pair to form groups of four. Finally, groups of four collaborate to refine their answers and share their responses with the whole class.

Find Someone Who: This activity is used to encourage students to seek out the students in class who know the answers to specific content questions.

Fishbowl: The fishbowl is a discussion format in which a small group of students sit in front of the class as a panel to discuss a topic while the remainder of the class observes. Afterward, discussion is opened to the whole class.

Five Whys: This strategy involves asking a chain or series of five "why questions," with each question delving deeper into the root or cause of a problem.

Focused Imagining: This is a form of guided imagery in which students are led to form mental images under the guidance of the teacher. This can be done either through written directions or step-by-step oral directions from the teacher.

Four Corners: In this strategy, the teacher labels the four corners of the room with "Disagree, Strongly Disagree, Agree, Strongly Agree." Students read a controversial statement and write on a piece of paper whether they agree, disagree, strongly agree, or strongly disagree with the statement and why. When students have finished writing, they go to the corner representing their points of view. Finally, students share their points of view with their group.

Grab Bag: Near the conclusion of a lesson, have a student draw an object from a bag. The student must explain or illustrate how the object is related to what they have learned.

Group Investigation: The class is divided into teams. Teams select topics to investigate, gather information, and prepare a report. Finally, the teams present their findings to the entire class.

Guided Practice: This is a form of scaffolding that gives learners an opportunity to attempt/try new skills with the support of the teacher before practicing independently.

Hands-On: This is an instructional activity that emphasizes students working with concrete objects or materials relevant to the content being studied.

Inductive Inquiry: This is a teaching method that models the process used in scientific inquiry. Steps usually include searching the literature, making observations, generating hypotheses, designing and carrying out experiments, analysis of results, and restarting the process.

Inquiry: Inquiry is a system in which students solve problems or answer questions by forming tentative answers (hypotheses) and then collecting and analyzing data to provide evidence for or against their hypotheses.

Jigsaw: This cooperative activity requires students to participate in a process that includes reading or learning specific material, meeting with expert groups, reporting back to the main team, and demonstrating knowledge through a test or report.

KWL: KWL stands for "What do you *know*? What do you *want* to know? What did you *learn*?" Students identify what they know about a topic, what they want to know, and after reading or instruction, they identify what they learned or would still like to learn.

Metacognition: Metacognition refers to a student's ability to "think about thinking." Learners monitor their own thought processes to determine if they are learning effectively.

Mind Map: This is a graphic way of organizing information to show the interrelationships between concepts.

Minute Papers: Students write briefly to answer the questions "What did you learn today?" and "What questions do you still have?"

Modeling: In this strategy, teachers model behaviors or skills.

Multiple Intelligences Theory: This is Howard Gardner's theory, proposing that each person has many intelligences (including linguistic, spatial, verbal, auditory, kinesthetic, musical, natural, and spiritual). These intelligences work together. Teachers should design instruction to foster the growth of all the intelligences.

Newsletters: Ask students to make suggestions or write parts of the class newsletter to be sent home to parents or a larger audience.

Pair Problem Solving: This is a problem-solving technique in which one member of the pair is the "thinker," who thinks aloud as they try to solve the problem, and the other member is the "listener," who analyzes and provides feedback on the thinker's approach.

Peer Editing: Students read and give feedback on the work of their peers. Peer editing is not only useful as a tool to improve students' analytical, literary, and communicative skills, but it also provides students with an alternative audience for their work.

Peer Tutoring: This strategy includes a wide variety of approaches in which instruction is delivered by a person close in age or achievement to the person receiving instruction.

Problem-Based Learning (PBL): PBL is an inductive teaching method without direct instruction. The teacher or a group of students poses an authentic (real-world) problem, and students learn particular content and skills as they work cooperatively to solve the problem.

Randomized Questioning: Students' names are written on popsicle sticks or note cards. After asking a question, the teacher randomly selects names of the students to answer the question.

Reader's Theater: Students adapt some of their reading to present to other students in the form of a dramatic presentation. These productions can be simple or elaborate, and they can include posters, programs, sets, and costumes.

Reciprocal Teaching: Students take turns being the teacher in a small-group setting. The teacher's roles include summarizing, clarifying, asking questions, and making predictions.

Scaffolding: This describes a process in which the teacher provides temporary support to the student until help is no longer needed. Scaffolding can take many forms, including giving examples, explanations, leveled text, and organizers. Effective scaffolding builds on student's existing knowledge and takes them to the next instructional level.

Socratic Method: This strategy involves leading students to an understanding through a succession of questions.

Think Aloud: A strategy in which the teacher vocalizes internal steps in problem solving or strategy use.

Think-Pair-Share: Students think individually, discuss their ideas with a partner, and finally, students share their ideas with the class or group.

Wait Time: The amount of time a teacher waits before accepting student responses is known as "wait time." How long a teacher waits after asking a question can influence the quality of responses provided by students. Increased wait time also leads to increased confidence in students and improvements in classroom discipline.

RESOURCE 6.2

Internet Sites by Content Domain

General Sources	
Kidsclick	http://www.kidsclick.org Web search for kids created by librarians at the Ramapo Catskill Library System—annotated list of sites with readability level included
Pics4Learning	http://www.pics4learning.com/ A copyright friendly image library for teachers
Web Quests	http://www.iwebquest.com/ Great resource for premade webquests as well as resources for designing your own webquests
KidSpace at the Internet Public Library	http://www.ipl.org/youth/ An Internet Public Library
Math	
National Library of Math Manipulatives	http://nlvm.usu.edu/en/nav/vlibrary.html A wide range of virtual manipulatives designed to reinforce skill acquisition and concept attainment
Rain Forest Math	http://www.rainforestmaths.com Interactive math activities K–6
Science	
American Museum of Natural History	http://www.amnh.org/ Includes areas on science, education, and kids and families
National Geographic for Kids	http://nationalgeographic.com/kids/ Bringing the world to your classroom
NASA	http://www.nasa.gov NASA for educators and students
Social Studies	
California State University, Northridge: Current Events and Electronic Resources for Kids	http://www.csun.edu/~hcedu013/cevents.html Resources for teaching current events
Library of Congress	http://lcweb2.loc.gov/amhome.html Primary sources for the classroom
National Geographic for Kids	http://nationalgeographic.com/kids/ Bringing the world to your classroom
National Park Service/Historic Places	http://www.nps.gov/history/ History Is Everywhere: Explore the National Parks

7

Assessing Student Learning and Performance

Assessment plays a vital role in education. It can vary from informal observations of students to the administration of formal, state-mandated standardized tests. Beginning with your first year, you will be required to understand and administer many forms of assessments. Some choices for assessing students will be up to you, and some will be required by your school, your district, and even the state in which you work. When the choice is up to you, selecting the best form of assessment is dependent upon having a clear understanding of you what you are trying to measure and what you plan to do with the results. In addition to measuring student achievement and growth over time, you will use assessment to inform and drive your instructional choices. Having a thorough understanding of the different forms and purposes of assessment will guide you in the best instructional choices.

TYPES OF ASSESSMENT

Assessment can be broadly categorized as either formal or informal. Each form has distinct advantages and disadvantages and is used for different reasons.

Formal Assessment

Formal assessments are standardized tests used to measure a student's aptitude, level of achievement, or performance relative to others of the same age or grade level. All formal assessments require a standardized protocol for administering, timing, and scoring. Formal assessments are often in the form of schoolwide, districtwide, and state-mandated tests. These can be further classified as either norm referenced or criterion referenced.

Norm-Referenced Tests

Norm-referenced tests are tests that have been "normed" or administered to a large group of students similar in age or grade level to those who will be evaluated. In this way, future results can be compared to the results of the "norming" population. Individual scores indicate a student's relative performance in a group. Scores from a norm-referenced test are reported in percentiles. A score of 70% indicates that a student scored better than 69% of those who took the test. This score does not mean that the student answered 70% of the questions correctly.

Criterion-Referenced Tests

Criterion-referenced tests measure what a student is able to do and what the student has mastered rather than indicating relative standing in a group. A student's score is compared against a predetermined benchmark or criterion. A score of 75% indicates that a student answered 75% of all questions correctly or a student has mastered 75% of the material included on the test. Many states have shifted from utilizing norm-referenced standardized tests to using criterion-referenced tests to measure student achievement. In this way, individual student scores can be compared to past performance to reveal growth in target areas.

Advantages of Formal Assessment

- Relatively easy to administer and score
- Students and teachers know what to expect—how the test will be administered and graded or scored
- Standardized procedures increase accuracy of results across testing sites

Disadvantages of Formal Assessment

- Reliance on multiple-choice format means that students are not challenged to create original responses
- Students cannot elaborate or add detail to answers
- Measures a broad base of understanding and not the depth of students' knowledge
- Provides little to no information for modifying classroom curriculum

Since the passage of No Child Left Behind (2001) most public and private schools rely on the use of standardized tests to measure student achievement and fulfill national and state accountability mandates. Many educators are worried that schools seem to be drowning in a sea of standardized tests. The trend seems likely to continue. Congress's recent decision to expand the National Assessment of Educational Progress (the "Nation's Report Card") and the movement toward new national education goals foreshadow an even greater emphasis on standardized tests. Proponents argue that a number of constituencies have a legitimate interest in the achievement levels of students and that they are entitled to accurate, adequate, and timely assessment data. Parents often request this information. In larger school districts, whole departments of specially trained evaluation experts coordinate and manage schoolwide assessment programs. As a beginning teacher, you will not have any say in the selection of tests to be administered on a schoolwide basis, nor will you have a say in their scoring or initial interpretation. Your main job will be to communicate test results clearly to parents and, perhaps, to upper elementary students themselves.

To communicate results effectively, you need to be aware of the limitations, criticisms, and objections to standardized tests. The criticism you are likely to hear most often is that multiple-choice tests focus on lower-level cognitive skills—that standardized tests are skewing the curriculum toward what is easily measured by machines: basic skills and isolated facts. School districts may require teachers to cover material because it is "on the test," and too much instruction is reduced to rote memorization and skill drills.

One major criticism of standardized tests is that they measure students' knowledge of standard English and test-taking skills as much as they measure content knowledge. Critics contend that the tests are biased in culture, race, and gender. Such criticism is especially significant when these test scores are used for tracking students into remedial or special programs.

You will probably be asked to review test scores with parents at conferences or explain test results that are published in a local newspaper to parents or students. Be prepared to discuss in nontechnical terms what norm-referenced and criterion-referenced tests are as well as their limitations. Focus parent attention on your own classroom assessment program that considers the prior knowledge of students, the classroom curriculum, and school benchmarks.

HIGH-STAKES TESTING

Throughout the nation, state-mandated standardized tests have become the centerpiece for standards-based school-reform efforts. These tests are "high stakes" because they are used as the basis for decisions regarding student placement, promotion, and graduation; teacher and administrator pay increases and bonuses; and individual school ratings and funding. Newspapers around the country now routinely rank local schools on the basis of students' standardized test scores. Despite cautions and caveats from testing experts, high-stakes tests have become the public benchmark of educational quality. The increased accountability that has accompanied reliance on high-stakes testing has profoundly affected the content of classroom teaching.

(Continued)

(Continued)

Unfortunately, the atmosphere of importance surrounding the exams can promote a success-at-any-cost attitude that brings out the worst in some schools. Whole subject areas are being omitted from the curriculum—art and music, especially, but also science and social studies in some cases—to make more time in the school day for teachers to prepare students for standardized tests. Instead of "teaching *toward* the test" and using assessment as an opportunity for thoughtful curriculum restructuring, some schools are actually "teaching *to* the test." This emphasis on the test, including repeated practice drills, may boost scores but can lead to rote teaching and disengaged learning. Good teachers in many areas are worried that their schools are focused more on accountability to the state or school district than to their students. Your job is to keep the purpose of standardized testing in perspective. Remember, it is only one form of assessment and does not paint a complete picture of an individual student's strengths or areas for improvement.

INFORMAL ASSESSMENT

While you most likely will have little to no choice in the selection and use of schoolwide, districtwide, or state-mandated formal assessments, you will be responsible for the assessment choices that you use in your classroom. As you begin to plan your lessons and curriculum, you will need to know your learners' areas of strength and weakness, so you can tailor your instruction to the needs of your students. You will also want to work with your grade-level team to be consistent with what assessments other teachers are using.

As a classroom teacher, you will be interested in where each student is on a continuum of learning. Children's learning tends to go through a series of phases, in spurts and splutters, as children accommodate new information, make connections among separate elements, and become able to construct abstract concepts or general principles. Informal assessments can be administered at any point throughout the year, thereby allowing you to adjust and modify your instruction to match the integrative, developing nature of children's learning. Informal assessments can include observation and anecdotal notes, checklists and rubrics, interviews, teacher-constructed tests, student portfolios, student-teacher conference notes, running records, and rating scales. Further, informal assessments can be both teacher administered or self-administered by students.

Performance-Based and Authentic Assessments

Many informal assessments are referred to as performance-based or authentic assessments. They seek to measure a student's ability to perform or complete a task in a specific subject area. The kinds of tasks used include essays, oral presentations, hands-on problems, and simulations.

The activities selected require students to demonstrate real competencies revealing what they know and what they can do. Performance-based or authentic assessments resemble real tasks and are categorized in three types: portfolios, performances, and projects. Examples include:

- Artwork
- Designs and drawings
- Experiments
- Maps
- Original scripts or plays
- Performances
- Problems solved
- Scale models

SUGGESTIONS FOR USING CLASSROOM PERFORMANCE-BASED ASSESSMENTS

Designing the Assessment

- Have a clear purpose in mind for the assessment; ask yourself how you will use the results.
- Devise tasks directly related to instructional goals that require students to apply what they have learned.
- Use tasks that have more than one correct answer or outcome.
- Use tasks that require more than one step to complete.
- Consider asking students to design their own questions, problems, or project.

Administering the Assessment

- Have students complete the assessment task during their regularly scheduled class time. More complex tasks may take a number of class periods and might include out-of-class work also. For such assignments, students should keep a log of their progress. Identify checkpoints at which you record pupil progress. This gives you a more comprehensive picture of student performance and enables you to diagnose weaknesses.
- Specify clearly what the students are to do and the parameters of the project.

Scoring the Assessment

- Avoid mental record keeping because you may forget important information about students' performance. Relying on memory can also result in your perceptions' being filtered as you observe subsequent students. Decide whether holistic or analytic scoring is appropriate on the basis of your purpose for the evaluation.
- Establish scoring criteria prior to using the assessment activity.
- Decide on a method of recording scores, and prepare the necessary materials, such as a checklist, rubric, or rating scale.
- Refer to a written copy of the scoring criteria when evaluating students' performance.

Classroom Observations and Anecdotal Notes

Experienced teachers know the value of observation as an assessment strategy. Careful, systematic observation is a critical tool for early assessment of student behavior, prior knowledge, strategy use, and ability. Taking time to record your observations in the form of anecdotal notes is equally as important. The notes you take become an important tool for understanding and evaluating the individual strengths and weaknesses of your students.

In the beginning of the year, create a logbook to maintain a record of your observations. Many teachers record behavioral or affective observations separate from observations related to academic progress. You may find it handy as you move about the classroom to carry a pad of sticky notes in your pocket to jot down observations, which can later be recorded in the logbook under the appropriate children's names. Be sure to check off names to ensure that you observe every student. Some teachers select a target student or students for the day. This strategy allows you to observe a single student in a wide array of contexts. By doing this, you will gain important information about your students, that may otherwise go unnoticed, that you might want to share during parent-teacher conferences. Additional suggestions for effective use of observation as an assessment tool include:

- Making a number of observations through time. One-shot observations are unreliable indicators of student stability or growth. By looking at children in many different instances, you can detect patterns, document growth, and spot areas that you can address through minilessons with a small group of students with similar needs.
- Knowing what you are looking for. To make effective observations, you need to be aware of developmental and academic expectations at your grade level: What learning strategies are appropriate for children of this age doing this task? (Refer to Resource 5.1, An Overview of Learning Objectives for Elementary Students.)
- Observe children in a variety of learning situations and settings—in whole groups, small groups, and individualized situations.

Written notes are only one way to document your observations. In addition, try using a tape recorder, iTouch, or other handheld recording device to capture children's story retellings and oral readings. Use a digital camera, videocamera, or FLIPcam to capture children working in pairs, groups, or interactive performances. Such documentation is wonderful to share with students to promote self-reflection. Giving students the opportunity to observe themselves in a social or learning situation fosters their ability to set personal academic or behavioral goals. Sharing this with families during conferences is an outstanding way of bringing your observations to life.

Rubrics and Checklists

A rubric is an authentic assessment tool used to evaluate student performance. It is based on a full range of criteria rather than relying on a single numeric score. While individual rubrics can vary according to the task, all rubrics share three common features. Rubrics:

1. Measure a specific objective;

2. Use a range to evaluate performance; and

3. Contain leveled performance characteristics describing the degree to which an objective was met.

While a wide variety of ready-made content-specific rubrics are available on the Internet, it is far more effective to create a rubric specific to the learning task you are assessing. Many teachers involve students in the process of creating rubrics. This strategy promotes critical thinking and enhances students' overall understanding of the parameters of a given assignment or learning activity. Use Resource 7.1 as a guide to creating rubrics for your particular grade level and learning activity. The advantages of using rubrics as an authentic assessment tool are many. Rubrics:

- Are easy to use and explain;
- Provide clear explanations of criteria used to judge performance;
- Enhance objectivity and consistency of evaluation;
- Foster self-assessment;
- Can be used as a guide to self-direct learning;
- Enable students to set goals for subsequent performance; and
- Provide informative feedback about individual strengths and areas for improvement.

Checklists differ from rubrics in that they do not contain leveled range-of-performance characteristics. In most cases, a checklist is a simple list of criteria or behaviors to be included or observed in a learning activity or performance. The overall simplicity and straightforward structure of a checklist make it a very efficient tool for assessing student performance. Checklists can range from a simple check-off list of specific criteria to be included in a learning activity to a more complex rating of criteria. Such checklists often include Likert-type rating scales (e.g., 1 to 5, or *seldom* to *often* ratings). Checklists can be a great way to assess the frequency in which a teacher observes specific student behaviors. Students can also learn to use checklists to assess whether they have completed all steps in a learning task or to monitor and assess learning and completion of tasks while working with partners or in small groups. (See Resource 7.2 for an example checklist.)

Questionnaires and Surveys

Questionnaires are very useful tools for understanding the beliefs and views of others. See Resource 7.3 for a parent questionnaire assessing students' self-perceptions, attitudes, and approaches toward learning. Understanding your students from their perspective gives you a greater insight and a more complete picture of each individual child. In addition, questionnaires can foster students' self-reflection. Having students complete questionnaires stimulates their ability to think about their own learning process.

Family surveys are another way to generate additional information about your students. Surveys allow you the opportunity to gather information about your student in general (see Resource 7.4) or about specific things, such as how much or how often children read outside of school, their favorite books or genres, favorite subjects, preferred learning styles, and individual family goals for the child. Keep in mind that checklists, questionnaires, and surveys are intended only as a beginning point in a comprehensive assessment program.

Interviews

Individual interviews with children can give you valuable information. An individual reading inventory (IRI) is a similar tool found to be useful by many elementary teachers. Consisting of graded word lists and story passages, an IRI provides an individualized, holistic assessment of a child's reading ability. Many large textbook publishers (e.g., Houghton Mifflin) provide a supplementary teacher's resource guide on how to conduct IRIs. If such a guide is unavailable in your district, an excellent resource is *Alternative Assessment Techniques for Reading and Writing* by Wilma H. Miller (1996). Interviews are also useful in gathering affective information about your students, such as what they like best about school, what is challenging for them, who their friends are at school, and what personal goals they have for themselves.

Teacher-Prepared Tests

One of the most traditional assessment activities, especially in the upper grades, is preparing written tests. A number of guidelines exist for teachers to follow as they construct their own classroom tests to measure student learning and assign grades for student work. The principles of test construction include making sure that test items match instructional objectives and curricular material taught and that questions are appropriate for the students.

Teacher-Made Tests and Quizzes

Custom-made tests prepared by teachers have a number of advantages when compared with commercially prepared tests. They can address learning goals unique to particular classes and grades, provide immediate detailed feedback, and are scored by teachers—which allows teachers to be more flexible in the way they perceive student answers.

As a student teacher, you probably developed quizzes and tests in subjects such as spelling, math, and social studies. Apply what you have learned about test construction as you write a rough draft of the test. After you have completed it, review the questions below as you check your work. Then, you will be ready to finalize, prepare, and administer your test.

- Are you including only those skills and concepts you have taught in class?
- Do you provide a variety of questions instead of presenting a single type, such as only true-or-false statements? Do some of your test questions encourage your students to apply concepts?
- Have you included a sufficient number of questions for students to answer? For example, include at least five examples focusing on the same concept, such as subtraction, in an arithmetic test. Establish how much time your students will need to take this test, and include the appropriate number of questions to be answered in a reasonable amount of time.
- Is this test only one of the many samples of work completed by individual students? Or are students' entire grades in a subject determined mainly by quizzes and tests?
- How will you plan for any absent students to make up tests? If students do poorly on the test, how will you reteach and assess again? What if some students do not complete the test because they need more time? What is your policy for retaking parts or all of the test if students performed poorly?

Formative Versus Summative Assessment

An important aspect of assessment is to predetermine the purpose of the assessment. Will it be used to inform subsequent learning and instruction or as a summative evaluation of student performance? Formative assessment is administered prior to or during a learning unit. Results from formative assessments indicate where students may require additional instruction and practice to master a specific skill or concept. Summative assessment is administered at the end of a learning unit and indicates how well a student has learned or acquired a new skill or concept. It is important to incorporate both forms of assessment into your comprehensive assessment program.

Additional Considerations
When Assessing Student Learning

Consider *why* you are assessing students, the purpose for the assessment, and the most appropriate assessment to meet your needs. Decide the following, lesson by lesson:

- Will it be graded?
- How will it be graded?
- Who will grade the lesson?
- When will it be graded?
- How will I use the grades?

Carefully explain to students how they will be graded and the quality of the work you expect. Use rubrics and models whenever possible.

Discuss with your mentor, grade-level team, or school principal any policies regarding late work, grade breakdowns, missed or incomplete homework and class work, and your school's grading systems (A–F or S–U). If your school uses letter grades, here is a traditional grading scale:

TRADITIONAL GRADING SCALE		
	97–100	A+
(95 percent = 4.0)	93–96	A
	90–92	A–
	87–89	B+
(85 percent = 3.0)	83–86	B
	80–82	B–
	77–79	C+
(75 percent = 2.0)	73–76	C
	70–72	C–
	67–69	D+
(65 percent = 1.0)	63–66	D
	60–62	D–
	59 and lower	F

Both formal and informal, continuous assessment of students' performance on a variety of measures is essential to good teaching!

Reporting Evaluations

There are many ways to let students and their parents know about progress made in school. Some of these ways include the following:

- Sending notes
- Checking and returning work
- Calling home
- Sending progress reports (these are in accordance with your school's policies and schedule)
- Holding teacher-parent conferences

Avoid using e-mail to report student progress. You may want to send an e-mail to inform parents that you will follow up with a phone call to share specifics.

TIPS FOR ASSESSING STUDENT LEARNING

- Have a procedure for evaluating and grading in place at the beginning of the year. You will need to explain this carefully to students and parents.

- Talk with your mentor or other teachers at your grade level to learn about assessment techniques commonly used at your school and school policies about assessment.
- Develop good observation skills, focusing on the whole child (social, emotional, physical, and academic).
- Be objective. Separate your emotions from the assessment process.
- Record exactly what you see or exactly what students do. Avoid temptations to infer, insinuate, judge, or inflate assessments based on your prior knowledge of student abilities. Always be as objective as you can.
- Keep an anecdotal record of specific student behaviors. (For example, "Jillian stared out the window for 10 minutes today during instruction." Or, "Arturo spoke out for the first time during reading group today.")
- Keep a folder for each student to file work samples, all correspondence to and from home, copies of student self-evaluation, and student anecdotal records.
- Refer to student cumulative records (cum file) to gather information such as age, family unit, previous teachers' comments, health, and referrals for special services.
- Talk with other professionals who come in contact with the student. Be careful not to be unduly influenced by comments, but learn as much as you can from other colleagues and professionals who have worked with this student.
- Develop methods for students to check papers occasionally. It is not necessary for the teacher to grade all assignments.
- Avoid giving unwanted "surprises" about student performance. Inform parents about assessment results in a timely fashion.
- Make sure students and parents understand your evaluation criteria. Go over expectations outlined in grading rubrics and/or what is required to earn each specific grade on a general grading scale (such as the traditional grading scale shown earlier).

Student assessment is a continuing, cooperative process among teachers, students, and parents. It begins the moment children walk into class on the first day. Assessment may not be your favorite activity as a teacher, but it is of utmost importance to parents and students. If done well, assessment will make a major contribution to your effectiveness as a teacher. It will help guide instruction, serve as information to report to parents, and fulfill requirements set by your school and district.

Portfolios of Student Work

Portfolios, a collection of samples of students' work collected through time, is an outstanding option for student assessment. Students examine and analyze their work and then decide with the teacher what items to include in their portfolios.

Some schools require students and teachers to work together in order to develop portfolios to both assess and demonstrate student achievements. The use of portfolios no doubt adds an additional dimension in assessing student performance. Be aware, however, that the implementation of an authentic assessment program using portfolios can be challenging for new teachers as well as for seasoned veterans. Most teachers are accustomed to more traditional assessment schemes that require less time and are more structured. In comparison with other forms of data collection and achievement tests, portfolio assessment can be cumbersome and time consuming.

Portfolio assessment, like other forms of assessment, must be an integral part of the instructional program because it will in part determine the kind of work students will complete. The purpose for keeping the portfolios must be clearly established at the outset for the stakeholders (teacher, students, parents, and administrators). Useful portfolios evolve from and are based on desired student outcomes. Portfolios are unique and insightful because they provide greater diversity in demonstrating student work, examining the depth and breadth of the big picture.

Portfolio Structures

Portfolios include a physical structure, such as chronological order, subject areas, and style of work and a conceptual structure, such as goals for demonstrating student learning. Classroom portfolios are simply varied collections of students' work. The collection is put into the portfolio by the student and the teacher. The container or holder can be an expandable folder, a box, or large file. It becomes a growing repository of the student's thoughts, ideas, and accomplishments.

Guidelines for Portfolio Development

1. Use the following guidelines to set up a portfolio system:

2. Determine which student work to include as well as which work to exclude (see the following sections, What to Put in Portfolios and Types of Portfolios). Most important, determine what constitutes excellent work through students' evaluation of their own work according to rubrics, checklists, or scoring systems that you and/or your students have developed. Decide what the purpose for the portfolio is—whether to showcase student work to families and classmates or strictly for evaluation.

3. Select student work samples at the end of a unit or quarter. Select a variety of daily and weekly student assignments. Have students write personal reflections or self-evaluations of their work samples to place in their portfolios.

4. Develop a cover letter that summarizes the types of information readers will find in the student portfolios. This enables you to use the portfolio to report to families and interested others. Monitor the frequency with which you examine portfolios by including a sheet that you initial and date at each viewing.

5. Remember that your students may need some time to become accustomed to the process of developing and maintaining their portfolios as well as evaluating their own work.

What to Put in Portfolios

Examples of work that other teachers and students have chosen to include in portfolios showcasing student work are listed below:

- Documentation of the writing process, including brainstorming notes made by the student, drafts, notes on additional ideas, and a final copy of the written work
- Other writing samples—prose and poetry
- Peer comments and review of student work, teacher reflective comments, and parent reflective comments
- Audio- or videotapes of the student reading aloud, oral presentations, and performances
- Cooperative group projects
- Graphs, charts, maps, diagrams, photographs, drawings, and computer-generated graphics
- Journals
- Autobiographies
- Interest inventories
- Solutions (with written explanations of how the answers were obtained) to math problems and science experiments

Types of Portfolios

Consider which portfolios would be most useful to you. One type of portfolio documents *processes* in learning and includes such items as

- Entry and exit skills, checklists, and pre- and posttests
- Anecdotal observations
- Multiple examples of classroom work selected by students and the teacher
- Records of individual conferences
- Oral reading on tape—early, middle, and end of year, and lists of books read
- Process examples (at least three) reflecting the writing process for the first and fourth quarters
- Math problem solving
- Science lab sheets from experiments

Another type of portfolio contains *best shot or showcase* examples, such as

- Final copies of "published" stories or poems
- Math and science projects
- Selected journal entries
- Audiotape of a polished book report presentation
- "Star" homework assignments
- Research paper
- Visual arts (drawings, paintings)

Most teachers choose to begin with *best shot* or *showcase* portfolios.

In summary, portfolios provide a cumulative record that shows student progress through time that is much richer in detail and substance than a mere list of scores. Students' work is placed in their portfolios at regular intervals. Portfolios not only can hold students' best work but also can represent evidence of student performance on a given range of categories or genres of work.

Portfolios can do the following:

- Assess outcomes as well as processes of learning
- Provide information that facilitates further effective instruction and learning
- Involve students in their own assessment by enabling self-selection and self-evaluation of work samples
- Result in more reliable evaluation by using more than one sample

Portfolios provide a number of benefits for students, including the following:

- Allowing students to observe their progress over time
- Increasing students' knowledge about the scope of what they have learned
- Promoting teacher-student interactions and collaborative learning
- Supporting student ownership and responsibility for learning

At the end of the year, get together with other teachers who want to know what your students have accomplished, particularly teachers who will have your students in their classes next year. Share your students' portfolios. In the meantime, discuss and review portfolios with individual students. Ask students to decide what work they wish to keep—perhaps their best, favorite, or most unusual.

RESOURCE 7.1

Rubric for Emergent Writers in Structure and Organization

I *Early Experimental*	II *Emerging*	III *Evolving*	IV *Knowledgeable*	V *Independent*
Writes letter strands, single words, or incomplete sentences	Writes short sentences using letter strands and CVC (consonant-vowel-consonant) spelling	Writes sentences using some sight words and CVC spelling	Writes short sentences using sight words and some correct spelling	Writes more complex sentences with correct spelling; uses a title
Begins to write using correct directionality	Writes consistently left to right and top to bottom	Sequences main events together	Attempts transitions between main events and ideas	Stories take on greater depth of meaning
Does not have a clear story sense	Story has some structure	Has a clear beginning	Has a beginning and an end with transitions in between	Has a clear beginning, middle, and end
Illustrates and uses dictation to tell the story	Inconsistent punctuation, capitalization, and spacing	More creative use of punctuation and more consistent spacing	Beginning sense of good sentence structure	Adds details and feelings to story

RESOURCE 7.2

Checklist: Assessing Language Arts in Your Classroom

	Yes	Some	Not Yet
Do you use a wide range of literature, different genres, and a variety of reading materials for read alouds and references?			
Do you have between 500 and 1,500 books in your classroom library and/or leveled library for students to use?			
Do your students have a regularly scheduled, daily independent reading time?			
Do you use shared reading and guided reading for small-group instruction?			
Do you implement student-teacher and buddy-student–buddy-student interviews/conferences for reading and writing?			
Do you schedule read alouds to your class daily?			
Do you plan and implement systematic reading and writing instruction?			
Is your reading and writing instruction driven by students' abilities and progress?			
Do you integrate technology into reading and writing instruction, modeling, and production?			
Do you integrate reading, writing, speaking, and listening into a balanced language arts curriculum?			
Do you provide opportunities for students to demonstrate their successes, such as Reader's Theater or author's chair?			

RESOURCE 7.3

Family Questionnaire About the Student

TELL ME ABOUT YOUR CHILD

My child's name is _____

My child's interests and/or hobbies include _____

_____

My child's special qualities include _____

My child's academic strengths include _____

My child's favorite subjects are _____

My child's greatest challenges are _____

_____

My child's areas of academic weakness are _____

My child approaches learning . . .

_____with excitement   _____with curiosity   _____with anxiety
_____with confidence   _____with reluctance

My goals for my child include _____

Questions or concerns that I have include _____

This survey will be strictly confidential. Thank you for helping make this a great year for your child.

RESOURCE 7.4

Survey: Examining Student Attitudes About Reading

Student Name: _____ Date: _____

Make one check for each of the questions for Strongly Agree, Agree, Disagree, or Strongly Disagree.

	Strongly Agree	Agree	Disagree	Strongly Disagree
I love to read.				
Reading is fun.				
I read because I have to.				
I read because I want good grades.				
I read to learn new things.				
I prefer to read to myself.				
I like to read with a friend.				
I like when someone else reads to me.				
I like reading fiction.				
I like reading nonfiction about real things, events, and people.				
I like mysteries.				
I like reading comics.				
I like poetry.				
I like adventures and fantasy.				
I like reading about sports and hobbies.				
I am a really good reader.				
Other kids are better readers than me.				
Reading is hard for me.				
I like to read to myself in my free time.				

RESOURCE 7.5

Summary Sheet for the Parent-Teacher Conference

CONFERENCE SUMMARY SHEET

Student: _____ **Date:** _____

Celebrations:

Concerns:

Social/Behavioral:

Written Language:

Reading:

Math:

Comments:

8

Developing Partnerships With Families

As a beginning teacher, you may feel that you have not have received sufficient training and information on dealing with the families of students. Yet, this is a crucial part of your job. Families need to be involved in their children's school life. Parent involvement in the education of their children is fundamental to effective teaching and academic success. Parent involvement improves students' achievement, students' attitudes toward learning, and students' self-esteem. Teachers who undertake strong comprehensive parent-involvement efforts and have strong linkages to the communities they serve are much more apt to have high-performing, well-behaved students. Parent involvement in children's education is more important to student success than family income or educational level.

The demographics of the American child have changed dramatically in recent years. (National Center for Education Statistics, 2009). Because families today are composed of more nontraditional configurations, children in our schools today live with parents, grandparents, other relatives, or unrelated guardians. They may come from single-parent homes, divorced homes, homes with same-gender parents, mixed ethnicities, mixed families with stepparents and stepsiblings, foster parents, unemployed parents, and adoptive parents. Some children are living in shelters or in transience. *Parents* is used in this chapter to refer to all primary caregivers.

Your goal is to build a trusting relationship with parents. In addition to traditional school events such as back-to-school night, open house, and parent conferences, find opportunities to develop regular communication with parents via phone calls and newsletters from the start of the school year. Schedule meetings throughout the year for which parents contribute to the agenda. Recognize parents for the positive things they do to help their children succeed. Project your belief that you also have much to learn—especially about your students as individual learners. Open up two-way communication, and invite parents to be your partners. It's worth the time and effort. Building positive home-school relationships will make a much smoother school year for you and for your students.

Although extremely important, developing partnerships with parents is not always easy. Some parents have attitudes toward school that make initial efforts at two-way communication difficult. Time and tact are necessary to enlist them as allies. Some parents feel intimidated by schools and may at first respond with sensitive, negative, or even hostile emotions. Some parents may think the school's values conflict with their own values or religious beliefs. Other parents may have busy work schedules that prevent them from participating in classroom activities. In some working families, it may appear that the babysitters are the primary caregivers. On the other hand, parents in a number of communities will be exceptionally interested, available, and ready to respond to your every request. Sometimes, you will find they are *too* available, and you may wish they had a job, too!

Seek to establish positive relationships with all the parents of your students at the start of the school year. It is of utmost importance to build the family-school partnership from the start. Open up communication. Most parents are willing to get involved in their child's class and help however they can, but it is up to you to contact them first. In some schools, you will get the class lists with ample time to call the student's home, introduce yourself, and welcome the family. Or, perhaps, if there is time, send a postcard to the student or an e-mail to the family. Welcome them to the classroom and to the school, especially if they are new to the school. If there is not time, consider calling home as early as possible to introduce yourself, and begin establishing positive interactions. By doing so, you are being proactive and setting a positive tone from the start.

If you are unfamiliar with the community in which you teach, particularly if you are in a smaller city or rural community, building positive community relationships is essential. Get to know as much about your new environment as you can. Drive around, go into the local stores, read the local newspaper, visit the library, police, fire station, post office, and introduce yourself. You will be delighted with the positive responses you receive!

Try to learn as much as possible about your new students and their families from last year's teachers, if possible. This is incredibly valuable information that is accessible to you ahead of time. For new students to the school, and for incoming kindergarten students, familiarize yourself with their files as much as you can in preparation for meeting them.

Today, many parents look to you to help with problems at home, such as getting ready in the morning, challenges with bedtime routines, mealtime, homework, and sibling rivalry. The more you cultivate and built trust and a solid partnership, the more they will support you and the work you do in the classroom.

GETTING TO KNOW PARENTS

Find out from your school principal, mentor, and colleagues the extents to which families are involved in your school and how other teachers in your school develop partnerships with parents.

Within the first few days of school, send a letter or e-mail home to each parent and/or student, welcoming the student into your classroom and briefly outlining expectations and needed supplies. First, find out if supplies are handled through your office or PTA. (Is there a student supply list that was sent home?) You can also let parents know your procedures regarding students' absences, homework, and your preference for parent-teacher communication (phone or e-mail). For parents of younger students and those new to your school system, they can be anxious and will want as much information as you can give them early in the year. Get contact information from parents right away. Their phone numbers and e-mails may have changed over the summer or since they registered. In addition to getting contact information from parents, let them know about school policies and procedures for things like morning drop off and afternoon pick up, riding the school bus, class supplies, snack and lunch, school uniforms if applicable, health and nutrition policies, and who has written authorization to pick up the student from school. Samples of such new-school-year letters are provided in Resources 8.1 and 8.2.

Hopefully, you will be assigned a parent-volunteer coordinator. This parent can help you with the scheduling of all your volunteers for both classroom and schoolwide events. Decide to what extent you want parents to participate on a daily basis in your classroom. As a general rule, you will want only one parent volunteer in the room at a time. Schedule volunteers for certain days in specific time slots. Most teachers prefer to have parents work directly with children. Remember *confidentiality!* You may not want parents correcting and filing papers, which would allow them to compare children's abilities and discuss it outside the classroom. Let parents know your expectations. They are there to help enrich instruction in the classroom. Some of the ways parents can assist in the classroom include:

- Reading with individual children;
- Supervising learning or interest center activities;
- Laminating and binding children's stories;
- Filing folders to go home, organizing portfolios, copying, and other class prep;
- Changing bulletin board displays; and
- Helping children with arts and crafts, cooking, or science projects.

Resource 8.3 is a sample letter asking for parent help and reminding them about issues such as confidentiality, no cell phones, what to do in the event the parent must cancel, and not to bring their child's siblings to the classroom during their volunteer time. Some teachers like to set up a meeting with all parents who will be volunteering in the classroom prior to parents starting. This way, the teacher can review all the expectations and policies. If you choose to use parents as volunteers, check school policies and informal norms about parents in the classroom. In many schools, parents need to sign in at the office and put on a nametag before working in the classroom. In other schools, parents need to be fingerprinted and have a background check.

As a rule, parent participation in schoolwide functions will vary. Discuss with your mentor which events specifically invite parents. Use a district calendar, your mentor and colleague's experiences, and your volunteer coordinator to highlight and plan for these regular activities. Examples include open house, back-to-school night, parent-teacher conferences, school music programs, fund-raisers, sports events, field trips, class parties, schoolwide events, book fairs, music performances, and grade-level parent meetings. Some teachers prefer to arrange their volunteers up until winter break in December rather than for the whole year. This allows teachers the flexibility to make any needed changes in the event there are any glitches with the schedule or certain personalities.

Before the opening day of school, ask your mentor or a teacher who knows some of your students to suggest the name of a parent who might be willing to volunteer in your classroom for at least the first few days of school and who might serve as your parent-volunteer coordinator. Call this parent, and ask if he would help get the year under way. Especially if you do not have an instructional aide, the parent helper can assist with the transitions during the first few days, helping students find their way around and generally assist you in getting off to a smooth start.

Plan to contact parents as frequently as you can during the school year, using e-mails or notices to inform them of important dates and information. Sending home student work keeps families informed of what you are working on in class. A weekly newsletter or "Friday Flier" is an excellent method of keeping parents informed of what is happening in the classroom. Include a brief summary of what the students did in language arts, math, technology, social studies, science, and perhaps in art, music, PE, Spanish, or other special classes. Include school events, reminders, dates to remember, and things to send to class.

Contacting Parents

Letters from the teacher to parents should usually be in formal typewritten form and should certainly be proofread. Some teachers prefer to send paper copies while others e-mail all correspondence. It is important to appear competent and professional, especially during your beginning years, when parents are still getting to know you. It is imperative that parents with limited English receive information in their primary language. Check with your site administrator for translators or bilingual teachers who can help you translate so that all families receive all teacher correspondence in their primary language. Always include your principal in group e-mails and letters. Most schools require that the administrator see all correspondence that goes out to parents. *Remember*, be very careful what you include in e-mail. E-mail is not protected. Be discreet. Think before you click send.

In addition to welcoming the students and introducing yourself, a first-day letter home can also inform parents about the following:

- Classroom rules and procedures
- Homework policies
- Plans and special events for the year

- Lists of ways parents can get involved
- Forms that must be returned to school
- An invitation to call or e-mail you at school with questions (include a phone number and e-mail address)

Give parents a media release form to sign that will give the teacher or others permission to take photos of students and post them in the room or anywhere in the school, in the class or school website, or local paper. Ask parents for permission to give class members their contact information. Give the dates for conferences, back-to-school night, open house, important dates, a school calendar, and your e-mail address. Send home a questionnaire to gather important information about the students. Find out if the student has any health needs or food allergies. Ask if there are any family situations you need to be made aware of (for instance, a restraining order or homelessness). Find out who has authority to pick the child up from school. Perhaps the parents have some special skills they would like to share with the class. Ask them about their hopes and expectations for their child for the year.

Check to see if a parent handbook is sent home to all new families from the school office. Coordinate your letter to harmonize with the amount of information that is provided by the school itself. Don't overwhelm families with too much information, but exchange important information right away. For families that do not return your forms, send them again. Be persistent. Perhaps they were lost or misplaced.

Many times, the best way to communicate with a parent is by phone. School phones may be used for such purposes. Before contacting parents, consider the following:

- What you will say (make notes in advance about what you would like to say, and keep the conversation focused)
- When you will call (decide the hour of your call)
- How you will sound (immediately put the parent at ease with a friendly tone)
- How to end the conversation (make an agreement and a plan to follow up, if necessary)

Oftentimes, meeting with a parent in person, if it can be mutually arranged, is more beneficial in order to establish a positive relationship.

In addition, if the purpose of your call is to set up a conference, consider beforehand exactly how you will ask the parents to come to school and meet with you. State the goals of the meeting. Describe the problem briefly and objectively. Indicate past efforts by you and/or the school to address the problem. Outline the proposed home-school collaboration. Reinforce any past support and willingness to confer. Make notes of what was agreed on, and let the parents know you are looking forward to the meeting.

DEALING WITH MANY DIFFERENT AND SOMETIMES DIFFICULT PARENTS

Building a good rapport and demonstrating positive communication skills early on will set the foundation for a good working relationship with your students' families. Parents' attitudes may differ toward your school and toward schooling in general. Often, parents' attitudes toward their child's school are a reflection of their own experiences in school, some of which may not have been positive. Some parents will naturally be easier to work with than others. Whatever attitude parents bring to school, it is your responsibility to establish and maintain a positive relationship with them. Often, poor attitudes reflect poor—or a lack of—communication between you and the parent. When communicating with parents, remember to

- Be patient;
- Be caring;
- Be compassionate; and
- Be a good listener.

Use active listening skills while speaking with a parent. Say, "I hear you saying . . ." Or, try to clarify what you hear them saying. In addition,

- Try not to get defensive;
- Report on observable behavior, not your opinions or speculations; and
- Try to be honest, kind, and respectful at all times.

Hopefully, the majority of your students' parents will be supportive, helpful, and kind. However, here are a few examples of the many types of parents with whom you might interact.

Aggressive

Many times, belligerent parents wish to address a perceived wrongdoing. Do not let their initial anger intimidate you. After greeting them politely, ask them to tell you what the problem is. Then, listen carefully. You may find that you are not really at fault. For instance, a beginning teacher had a first-grade student who typically arrived at school an hour late. The teacher set up a conference with the parents to discuss the tardiness problem. The teacher didn't realize that the parents felt threatened and angry at being asked to come to school to discuss it.

Such a situation takes every bit of your diplomacy and tact. But don't back down. In this case, the teacher felt that chronic tardiness was a serious problem needing to be discussed in a forthright manner. The teacher explained to the parents her belief that the child was missing important parts of school that affected her learning, and that the tardiness was disruptive to the class. The parents expressed that to them it was unimportant exactly what time the child arrived. They were able to "hear" the teacher's sincere conviction that school, even first grade, is important and requires a commitment by everyone—the student, the parents, and the teacher. The teacher's sincerity, concern, and care not to blame the parents turned a potentially difficult situation into a healthy one. The teacher asked the parents to help get the child to school before the tardy bell and expressed support for their efforts. The next week, when the student arrived on time several days in a row, the teacher wrote the parents a note appreciating their efforts and describing how their child was enjoying and participating in the morning circle activities in a special role as calendar monitor.

Indifferent

Indifferent parents appear to have little or no interest in their children's schoolwork or activities. They rarely come to school or return necessary forms on time, if at all. When you try to contact them by phone or notes, you wait a long time for a reply, or worse, you hear nothing at all. You may feel tempted to end further efforts to get in touch with these parents. It is important to maintain contact through notes, memos, and calls, however, even if you do not hear back from them. In the meantime, verify information such as telephone numbers and addresses with your school's main office. Let your mentor and principal know about your efforts to contact this child's parents and the results. Keep a record of your attempts because occasionally you need to refer to these records at a later date. Sometimes, there may be reasons for the parent's apparent indifference. They could possibly be intimidated by the school or not understand the importance of your notes and calls. Perhaps, they are not indifferent at all. Language or home issues may prevent them from responding to you in a timely manner.

Reluctant

Reluctant parents are ones that do not share a lot of information with you, and you do not frequently hear from them as often as you would like. You wish you had more opportunity to talk with them about their children's progress or lack thereof. Sometimes, students may volunteer information about their home situation that sheds light on your difficulty in establishing two-way communication with their family. There may be sensitive issues that the parents are reluctant to share with you, such as problems at home between the parents, joblessness, homelessness, or transience. Be sensitive and patient. Let the family know you care while being sensitive to their privacy. Nevertheless, do not give up on your attempts to involve these families.

Cooperative and Interested

These parents are usually a joy to work with. They return requests for information promptly and assist whenever asked. They appear generally interested in their child's education and have a positive attitude toward school and your classroom. One or two of these parents can be recruited as class volunteer coordinators who serve as liaisons between you and the other parents. They can be of tremendous help to you, coordinating and arranging activities such as volunteer schedules and school events, planning class celebrations, driving for field trips, and organizing fund-raising. Thank them frequently, and let them know you appreciate their efforts!

Anxious

These parents are also cooperative, interested, and fairly easy to work with; but in some cases, they seem to be overly concerned about the specifics of their child's social or academic progress. Perhaps there is a valid reason. There may be family issues that the parents feel may impact their child's behavior in school. Sometimes, children are experiencing difficulties at home of which you are unaware. Make an effort to invite the parents for a conference to address their concerns and share their knowledge of their children. If there is a problem, you will have an opportunity to help solve it.

In conclusion, many parents today, unfortunately, because of work and other commitments, lack the time or opportunity to get involved in their children's school as much as you or they might like. They still care deeply for their children, however, and desire a quality education for them. Let all parents know how much you value and encourage their support and participation in this important part of their children's lives. Anticipate that they will respond in a positive way and in any manner they can. Continue to maintain open communication, an honest exchange of expectations, and invite them to keep you informed of important events in their children's lives. You can look forward to a rewarding partnership and a smooth school year.

CONDUCTING PARENT CONFERENCES

Before the Conference

The parent-teacher conference is the most commonly used means of sharing information between the home and the school. Many schools schedule two regular conferences per year, fall and spring, to coincide with report card periods. Often, one specific day or a series of minimum days are set aside each year for conferences. Individual conferences can vary from 15 to 30 minutes. Some teachers like taking more time. Try scheduling them, if possible, strategically so that conferences that may need to go longer can do so without making other parents wait. Check your school policy regarding these annual conferences. Of course, you can schedule additional conferences with parents as needed. Try to accommodate working parents as best as you can, meeting them before or after school. Try to encourage both parents, if possible, to attend. You will get a different picture of the student with more family input.

Inform parents ahead of time about the purposes of the conference. A sample letter to send home prior to your meeting is provided in Resource 8.4.

Be prepared to listen. Parents often come with their own concerns. Asking an open-ended question at the beginning of the conference about how things are going for the student gives parents the opportunity to express their interests and concerns. Many of your parents and students will have different ethnic, cultural, religious, family, and socioeconomic backgrounds than your own. If English is a second language to a student's family, invite another family member, relative, or close friend who can translate for you—unless you are fluent in their primary language. Help them feel welcome and comfortable. If day care is a problem, invite siblings into the class to play while you meet. If parents do not sign up for a conference, keep trying. Offer alternative times and dates. If nothing else, hold a telephone conference. If you think there will be a difficult conference, invite your principal or another teacher (a resource specialist perhaps) to join you. Or, try scheduling a colleague to come into your room at a certain time in order to check on you or to get you out of a very long and uncomfortable conference.

Some teachers request students to participate in conferences. It can be helpful, especially if there are behavior problems to resolve. This can help clear the air and ensure that everyone understands the expectations. Students who are doing well enjoy participating in the exchange of the conference, as well. Check with your colleagues to see how conferences are held at your school.

Find out what you can about the child's history *before* the conference. Review cum files, former teachers' notes, social and discipline history, referrals for testing, past standardized test results, and report cards. Changes in family structure such as divorce, death, birth, and so on, are also critical to be informed of ahead of time.

Be prepared with ideas for parents to help their children at home. For example, prepare handouts of curriculum outlines, grading procedures, homework criteria, and any instructional materials you want sent home. Share a list of upcoming projects that would benefit from parent monitoring and assistance. You will handle this differently depending on the student, the parent, and the material. Have a list of good books your students can read alone or parents can read to them. If you choose to have parents work with their children on particular skills, provide them with specific directions and materials. (See Resource 5.3 for a list of outstanding read-aloud books.) Also, share suggestions of appropriate activities and enrichment opportunities that might benefit the child—perhaps after-school sports, art, music, science camps, museums, and libraries—always being sensitive, however, to each family's ability to pay.

If you plan to share standardized test scores with parents, be ready to explain what these scores indicate, as well as what they are *not* intended to mean. Your district may have a policy on this. Check it out ahead of time.

Have samples of each student's work ready. Dated samples show growth and improvement and help provide specific information for parents and direction for the discussion. Avoid comparing the student's work with that of other students. Mention something about each student's strengths as well as areas that need improvement.

During the Conference

Think about the four purposes of a typical conference: information getting, information giving, joint problem solving, and development of mutual trust. In order to do this, listen, ask questions, show the student's work, and then discuss it.

Collect all needed materials for each child in a folder or portfolio, ready on a table. Work samples speak for themselves and paint a picture of what you are trying to explain. Side-by-side seating (instead of your sitting behind your desk) is less formal and less intimidating to most parents. Set a positive climate by welcoming them with a smile and a friendly voice and establishing a feeling of caring and collaboration. Set out paper and pencils, so they can take notes. Keep notes of main points you will want to remember, too.

To start the conference, consider first asking the parents how things are going for their child. What does their child say about school? What do the parents share that may shed light on academics or behavior? Often, your perspective is changed when you understand the family's expectations.

Seek parents' input. Discussing the child's strengths first helps relax ill-at-ease parents. Encourage them to tell you what they expect of their child, of you, and of your school. Their facial expressions, gestures, and tone of voice can provide clues concerning their feelings for their child. Always give parents the chance to express possible reasons for a child's poor work or misbehavior in the classroom, explore the possibilities together, and discuss strategies that might help the child. Thank them for their helpful insights. Use language to which parents can relate, but be positive and professional too. Do not label or diagnose. Report on observable behavior only. Check with your administration before you begin suggesting tutoring, counseling, or testing. It may be a policy of the school not to suggest it without being held responsible for providing or paying for it.

Conversely, do not let a parent berate you. If a parent becomes verbally abusive, simply say, "I do not think that the purposes of this conference are being met. Perhaps we can schedule another conference date." Never argue with parents. The next conference should be scheduled to include your principal and/or union representative. If you expect a difficult conference, ask the principal or a more appropriate person, such as the special education director or the vice principal, to sit in.

During the conference, avoid negative expressions, such as *trouble-maker*, *lazy*, and *sloppy*. Instead, substitute positive suggestions and/or specific descriptions of the behavior in carefully worded language. Rather than "sloppy," you might say, "could do neater work"; rather than "lazy," "has a chance to earn a higher grade"; rather than "hyperactive," "often out of seat without permission"; and so forth. Stick to your schedule during the conference day or evening, especially if other parents are waiting. Ask if you can schedule another time and date to finish up loose ends.

You may need to set up a special conference to focus on a specific problem situation as needed. Your purpose in this type of conference is to define and clarify an issue and make plans to solve it. Here are some tips to make this sort of problem-solving conference go more smoothly:

- Tackle only one problem at a time—don't try to change everything at once!
- Choose what seems to be the most critical problem.
- Refer to records and notes to support the issue.
- Outline the proposed home-school collaboration.
- Plan for follow-up. For example, will you send home a daily report, and will the parents return the completed form to you?
- Set up another formal or informal time to check in. Follow up.
- Make agreements and responsibilities extremely clear at the end of the conference. Write them down. Give parents a copy.

End the conference on an upbeat, positive note. Let the family know how much you appreciate their time and involvement and how much you enjoy having their child in your class. If you have agreed to find out information for the parent or send information home, add it to your To Do list, and keep your word.

Whether the conference was a regular school event or a special meeting to discuss a problem, spend a few moments afterward to assess its effectiveness. Ask yourself the following questions:

- How well prepared was I?
- How well did I use time?
- Did I start on a positive note?
- Did I listen attentively?
- Did I involve the parents?
- Were follow-up plans made, if needed?
- Did I gain any insights?
- Are there new interventions I need to implement?

BACK-TO-SCHOOL NIGHT AND OPEN HOUSE

In most schools, your first formal introduction to parents will be in the form of some sort of "meet the teachers" event, such as "September Open House" or "Back-to-School Night." To prepare, talk with colleagues to find out what parents at your school normally expect from this session, how many parents you might expect in attendance, and in what form teachers present (PowerPoint presentation, Smartboard, handouts, etc.).

In some schools, a back-to-school night is held in the fall, and an open house is scheduled in the spring to showcase what your students have been doing all year. If your school does not schedule these events, consider holding a parent-orientation meeting in September just for your own class for the purpose of introducing yourself and informing the parents about your class and the year's highlights.

Back-to-School Night

Traditionally, back-to-school night has been a schoolwide event at which teachers inform parents of their classroom philosophy, behavior expectations and discipline policies, daily schedules, academic programs, homework policies, parent communication, and so forth. In most cases, the teacher talks almost every minute of the allocated hour.

Promote the concept of parents as partners in the education of their children. Here are some suggested goals for you. Inform parents you intend to:

- Build relationships with and among parents; and
- Build a strong home-school connection in which parents feel like partners in their children's education.

Preparing for back-to-school night is demanding and exciting. Just as for the opening day of school, you should be *overprepared*. Because you are a first-year teacher, many parents may be coming to "check you out." Your classroom should be spotlessly clean and organized, with bright bulletin boards and student work on display. Make an effort to hang as much student work as possible in the classroom. Place additional work in special folders or booklets on each student's desk. Encourage parents to sit at their child's desk. Give parents nametags to fill out. Parents enjoy looking through their children's accomplishments, and this gives any early birds something to do. Make sure that you have names on all desks and that students have cleaned their desks inside and out.

Write the daily schedule on the board, so parents can actually see what their children do each minute and hour they are at school. Have a sign-in sheet ready for parents (your school may require this) and a welcome sign outside your classroom door with the room number and your name. Set out extra chairs for students who participate that night and for grandparents or additional adults who attend.

Agenda

Carefully plan your agenda for the evening. (See Resource 8.5 for a sample back-to-school night agenda.) Not only must your classroom look great, but also you must be well organized.

1. Welcome (warmly greet parents and introduce yourself)

2. Get-acquainted activity (optional, depending on time available)

3. Parents as partners:
   o Let parents know that you see them as important partners in their children's education and that you want to learn what their expectations are for the year.

4. Teacher's presentation of goals and classroom educational program:
   o Here, you have the opportunity to communicate your sense of purpose as an educator. Be sure to emphasize that you have high expectations for the academic success of each child. Instead of giving parents a list of policies and schedules, share the heart of your program with them. Focus on curriculum and highlights of the year.

5. Question-answer period:
   o Allow several minutes to answer specific parent questions. If some parents tend to monopolize the time (often with questions about their own children), say, "Our goal tonight is to overview the instructional program, but I would be happy to meet with you for an appointment at another time." Let parents know your door is always open. Some teachers talk right to the end to avoid questions and answers. It's your choice!

6. Homework and discipline policies:
   o These policies are fundamental to share with parents. Instead of presenting them in detail, consider preparing a handout of these important items that you will not have time to go into extensively during the presentation.

7. Continuing communication and volunteers:
   o Let parents know that you will be communicating with them throughout the year and that they are always welcome to send you a note, give you a call, send you an e-mail, or make an

appointment. Let them know how to contact you. Write the school phone number and your e-mail on the board. Some teachers give their home number, too. Ask your colleagues how they typically communicate with parents. Use the evening as an opportunity to recruit volunteers. Provide a sign-up sheet.

Open House

Preparations for open house in the spring (usually May) are similar to those for the back-to-school event in the fall. Rather than introducing parents to your curriculum and expectations, however, the major goal in a spring open house is celebrating students' accomplishments. Make your classroom come alive with student projects and displays. Showcase major reports and projects completed by your students several weeks prior to open house night. The spring of the year is an especially good time to have students take an active role in planning and presenting the open house program for their parents. Have students write invitations to their parents. Prepare a checklist so that all children can serve as tour guides, explaining the year's highlights to their parents. Include writing samples, technology (software the students use, technology projects they have made, a slide show, a movie), math projects, evidence of science learning, social studies, and other areas. Make open house an interactive and engaging learning experience for students and their families.

BUILDING A CLASS COMMUNITY

Try to make families feel that their child's class is an important part of their lives. Create a welcoming, supportive environment in which they feel included. Encourage parents to participate in class and school events. Have your volunteer coordinator help organize a class picnic at the beginning of the year for families to meet each other. Include grandparents and other significant family members. Once families have agreed, give them each other's phone numbers and e-mails, so they can begin communicating with each other and set dates up for their children to play after school. Celebrate at the end of the year together with another party or picnic. You will be surprised to see how close the families have become through the year.

RESOURCE 8.1

Sample New-School-Year Letter to Parents of Primary Children

Send a hard copy and also e-mail.

Date: _____

Dear Parents,

Welcome to the new school year! I am so happy to have your child in my class this year. I am looking forward to a fantastic year! We have so many wonderful things planned for the year, and we are off to a great start! During the last two days, we have met our classmates, toured the campus, learned many procedures in class (such as checking out books from our class library, being a class helper, transitioning to recess, lunch, and specialists), and we have had a class meeting to establish our class rules. We have jumped right in with writer's workshop, our math and science units, and we have visited our specialists and learned all about our daily schedule. The following are a few suggestions:

1. Put names on all materials your child brings to school.

2. Please pack your child a healthy snack each day.

3. Put names inside any clothing that your child might take off and could be easily misplaced.

4. Have a set bedtime on school nights, so that your child is not tired in school.

5. Establish a good time for your child to read at home, and establish a good homework place free of distraction (if possible), and designate a good time to get homework accomplished.

I have enclosed a class schedule so you will know when the students have PE, music, art, technology, and Spanish.

Please mark your calendars for September _____, for our annual back-to-school night. I will look forward to meeting you and giving you lots of information about the school year at that time.

I am looking forward to meeting and working with all of you. If you need to contact me, the best way to contact me is through e-mail. My school e-mail address is _____. I am available at school from 7:30 a.m. to 3:30 p.m. daily. You can leave me a message through my classroom phone (phone number). Please know I will return your calls and e-mails within 24 hours.

Cordially yours,

RESOURCE 8.2

Sample New-School-Year Letter to Parents of Children in Elementary School (Grades 3–5)

Date: _____

Dear Parents,

A new school year is here, and I would like to take this opportunity to tell you that I am excited about it—and I hope your child is, too. Fifth grade is an exciting learning year. Children begin to progress rapidly and pick up new ideas quickly.

The daily schedule for the fifth grade is as follows: I will teach reading, English, spelling, creative writing, and social studies (science will replace social studies in the second semester) to your child every day. From 12:05 to 1:00 each afternoon, the fifth graders will go to Mrs. _____'s room for math. Mrs. _____ is currently on maternity leave and is being replaced by Mrs. _____ for approximately six weeks. This schedule will help the children get used to having more than one teacher but also provide the benefits of having a homeroom.

Please take a moment to look over the notes and papers your child brings home each day, and remember to look for the Friday folder that will be sent home each week containing the work your child has completed and other important information.

I am looking forward to getting to know you and your child better. Please make every effort to attend the back-to-school night on September 22 at 7:30 p.m. If you have questions before then, please feel free to call the school at _____ and leave a message. I will get in touch with you as soon as possible.

Once again, I am looking forward to an exciting year with a lot of learning taking place. I will see you at back-to-school night on September 22.

Sincerely,

RESOURCE 8.3

Sample Letter Asking for Parent Volunteers

Date: _____

Dear Parents,

Thank you so much for your willingness to be a part of our school day! We welcome parent volunteers as an important partnership in the home-school connection. We welcome you into the classroom!

Before you begin a shift in our classroom, please sign in at the office, and get a volunteer badge. Please remember to turn off your cell phone, and be aware that we are not able to accommodate siblings while you are working in the classroom.

You will be working with our students during centers, or you may be working on cooking, art, technology, science, or writing projects.

If you are unable to keep your designated day in the class, please try to have another parent cover for you.

Confidentiality is very important in our classroom. You will observe many different learning styles, abilities, and behaviors. Please respect confidentiality of information about students. Refrain from discussing individual children outside of the classroom.

We look forward to your time in the classroom with us this year. Thank you for your time, effort, and energy in volunteering.

Sincerely,

RESOURCE 8.4

Sample Parent-Teacher Conference Letter

Date: _____

Scheduled conference date and time: _____

Dear Parents,

In preparation for our conference next week, I would like to take this opportunity to inform you of what we will be discussing. Because of the limited time we have scheduled, it would help if I knew what questions and concerns you have ahead of time. There is some space below to jot down any questions or concerns that you might have. Either send them back to school with your child, or bring them with you when you come to the conference.

When we meet, I'll be talking about:

1. How your child is performing overall in school. We will also review your child's progress report (if applicable).

2. Our curriculum with samples of your child's work in reading, writing, and math.

3. Your child's academic strengths and areas for growth.

4. Your child's social interactions with classmates.

5. Any other concerns or areas for discussion.

You probably have some things that you want to talk about, too, your expectations, and perhaps some questions about your child. Please take a few minutes and write those below.

Areas I would like to discuss:

_____

_____

_____

What I hope my child gains in school this year:

_____

Thank you for your help.

Cordially,

RESOURCE 8.5

Back-to-School Night Agenda

1. Welcome

2. Classroom philosophy and expectations

3. Daily and weekly schedules

4. Curriculum:
    o Language Arts
    o Math
    o Science
    o Social studies
    o Technology
    o Foreign language, music, art, PE, library, health

5. Character development and conflict resolution

6. Parent-teacher communication, conferences, and parent volunteers

9

Your Own Professional Development

The craft of teaching is a lifelong process. Successful teachers grow in effectiveness throughout their professional careers as they gradually overcome challenges, develop strengths and confidence, and hone their style and strategies. Beginning teachers often feel as if daily teaching responsibilities totally consume their lives. New teachers typically report thinking about their students and teaching commitments every waking hour. They even dream about them!

You undoubtedly are working hard to ensure a positive, flourishing year for your students. As they grow, so can you. You have needs as a learner, too. Don't neglect your own professional growth and development.

The educational profession is constantly changing as research-based practices and strategies are developed to improve both instructional methods and student outcomes.

For now, however, concentrate on what you need to learn as you become more confident in your ability to teach effectively. Learn through personal experience, trial and error, reflection, critical inquiry, and problem solving about situations in your own classroom.

REFLECTING ON YOUR PRACTICE

When you reflect on your experience, you have an opportunity to grow from it. Keep notes of what worked and what didn't. Jot down notes in your lesson book or schedule where you can refer to them later or even the next year. Develop a habit of analyzing what you do and why. Monitor your decisions about what and how you teach and how you interact with children. Evaluate your successes as well as your weaknesses. Contemplate what works to engage students in learning. As you consider alternative courses of action, you'll expand your teaching repertoire and refine your approach for the next time. Look back thoughtfully and accurately to assess your effectiveness. Define what specific strategies were successful, and begin to apply those to other instructional situations. Learn from your mistakes, and grow from self-evaluation. Let these insights serve as springboards for discussions and new discoveries. If you merely survive your first year of teaching without thinking closely about it, you will miss profound opportunities to examine and savor your experiences.

Becoming an accomplished teacher is a complex process. No matter how well you learn to execute specific teaching methods and procedures, building a repertoire takes time. One productive way to reflect is *out loud,* talking with a mentor or a peer. Mentoring is really just one teacher facilitating the growth of another. Collaboration and reflection with a supportive listener may be your best source of information and emotional succor. From this, you will learn, grow, and gather strength to be a truly professional teacher.

Keeping a journal of your personal reflections and self-assessments is also valuable. Despite the constraints of classroom life, a certain degree of reflection is possible. Continue to ask yourself how you might do things differently if they do not go as well as you expected. A good idea is to write in your journal whenever you have students write in theirs. You will be modeling good writing habits while giving yourself a lull in the action and a chance to record events and personal reactions. Sometimes, the simple act of writing about an issue will clarify it for you. What happened? Why did it happen? What was my role? What beliefs did my actions reflect? How should I act in the future? Reflection will give you perspective on events.

Asking a colleague to videotape you while you are teaching is another way to reflect on your teaching methods. While watching the video, ask yourself whether you noticed any habits you would like to break. What was your body language communicating? Was your voice clear, positive, and upbeat? Was your face happy and enthusiastic? Developing the habit of reflecting on your practice is one of the best (and cheapest) professional development activities available.

Thinking About Teachers as "Professionals"

American teachers have an image problem. As teachers, we are members of one of the largest, most complex, and most important professions in this country. Yet, true professional status eludes us. In many cases, teachers simply are not viewed or treated as professionals—by the public, by school and district administrators, by parents, or even by themselves. The issue of professionalism is a critical ingredient in this country's efforts to improve education. Professionalism, public confidence, and school improvement are important interlocking pieces.

A *professional* is universally defined as someone who has mastered the ability to make informed judgments and perform important tasks in complex environments. The decisions, performances, and judgments professional make are grounded in a research-based and empirically supported foundation of knowledge.

Teachers certainly fit this definition. They apply their knowledge of students and classrooms in deciding when, what, and how to teach. Even in the most routine situations, teachers must make multiple and simultaneous judgments. They must continually gather and organize large amounts of information and juggle several sometimes contradictory goals. The unique structure and expectations of your school frequently dictates the parameters of *what, when,* and *how* you are expected to teach. Your individual style, background experiences as a student yourself, and your own beliefs and philosophy of education also impact your instructional methods, time spent on subjects, and curriculum.

As a new teacher, you stand at a pivotal time as a teaching professional. The *art* of teaching is swiftly transforming into the *science* of teaching. Currently, researchers are systematically examining teaching in a scientific manner and reporting on the positive effects of instruction on student learning and outcomes.

In previous decades, the belief that schools made little difference in the achievement of students was widespread. The vast majority of differences in achievement were attributed to factors such as the student's natural ability, aptitude, "intelligence," the socioeconomic status of the school, and the student's home environment. Unfortunately, this attitude devalued the teacher's professionalism.

Recently, the myth that teachers do not make a difference in student learning has been refuted. It is now recognized that the teacher's role has strong implications for student achievement and overall academic success. The teacher-student relationship, instructional approaches, differentiation of instruction, understanding of different learning styles, and respect for individual and cultural differences have all been found to have strong influences on students' overall academic success. Although home environment, parents' education and participation in the students' learning, socioeconomic status, and ethnic and cultural differences have been found to contribute to children's behavior and academic success, the individual classroom teacher is now recognized to have even more of an effect on student achievement than originally thought. In fact, many educators agree that the most important factor affecting student learning is the teacher. The immediate and clear implication of this finding is that improvement in the overall effectiveness of teachers can lead to improved educational outcomes for students.

Teachers *do* make a difference! Keep this in mind as you grow as a professional and master the complexities of schools and classrooms. While you may, at times, get discouraged, frustrated, and question your abilities, remind yourself that you do make a difference. Take pride in knowing that the commitment of new teachers is perhaps the most powerful resource for change that exists in public education today.

JOB-EMBEDDED, SITE-BASED PROFESSIONAL DEVELOPMENT

Our current understanding of the impact an effective teacher can have on student performance has led Learning Forward (formerly the National Staff Development Council) to propose amendments to the Elementary and Secondary Education Act (National Staff Development Council, 2001). This proposal includes both a new definition of quality professional development along with specific standards for implementation. The new standards will broaden the professional development path you will take throughout your career. In addition to participating in conventional models of individualized professional development commonly referred to as workshop-driven professional development (discussed later in this chapter), you also will participate in collaborative, job-embedded professional development. This is good news for you as a teacher new to the profession.

Learning Forward defines professional development as a "comprehensive, sustained, and intensive approach to improving teachers' and principals' effectiveness in raising student achievement" (Hirsch, 2009, p. 12). Under this new definition improving student performance is the collective responsibility of collaborative teams and not the sole responsibility of the individual teacher. These teams may be referred to as "Communities of Practice" or "Professional Learning Communities." Under this new definition, professional learning and development

- Is aligned with local and state academic standards for students;
- Occurs several times a week among teams of teachers, principles, and other staff members; and
- Is conducted at the school site and is facilitated by mentor teachers, coaches, principals, master teachers, or teacher leaders.

The core belief behind the new definition is that all teachers *can* learn and *should* learn, and the most powerful form of professional learning occurs when teams of teachers meet on a regular basis to analyze student achievement through a broad array of data, plan lessons, problem solve, and establish both teaching and learning goals. No matter how such teams are labeled at your new school, the good news is that you are not alone—you are a member of a professional learning community (PLC).

PROFESSIONAL DEVELOPMENT THROUGH IN-SERVICE AND GRADUATE STUDY

In addition to implementing a PLC model of professional development, many school districts sponsor induction workshops and seminars to benefit beginning teachers. Take advantage of these opportunities to gain mentoring support and to establish a professional network with other beginning teachers in the school system. You will find useful and practical ideas about managing student behavior, engaging students in active learning, and using instructional materials and resources.

Other in-service workshops and trainings may be offered for *all* teachers at your school, district, or at the county level. These programs are scheduled when teachers are available to attend—usually on minimum days (when students have a short school day) or in the late afternoon. Evening workshops covering a wide array of diverse topics are often offered for teachers interested in participating outside of school hours. In-service workshops are often led by veteran teachers with expertise in special curriculum areas. At other times, the topics covered in these workshops can be as varied as time management, behavior management, conflict resolution, health and nutrition, violence in the schools, or other current issues of importance. Workshops you are required to attend during the school day are paid for through your school district. Always check first with your administrator before registering for conferences or workshops to clarify who is paying, and whether or not you are eligible to receive credit for these classes.

Taking continuing education classes at a college or university, or pursuing a master's or doctorate degree, is an outstanding way of continuing your professional development. Explore advanced degrees in your teaching subject, in curriculum and instruction, in counseling, or in educational administration. Most school districts provide pay increases on the salary schedule for teachers who earn graduate credit units and degrees. When pursuing these classes, always check first with your administrator to clarify how it will affect your salary, and whether or not the school district will contribute toward your tuition. Also, look into local grants and scholarships that may help fund your continuing education.

PROFESSIONAL DEVELOPMENT THROUGH REGIONAL AND NATIONAL CONFERENCES

To keep abreast of current research in education and related fields and to recharge yourself with new inspiration, attend every convention and conference you can. These professional meetings are important ways for beginning teachers to feel less isolated and more empowered, and they will expand your awareness and knowledge base. The intellectual stimulation will help enable you to make informed choices.

In your search for professional growth opportunities, join at least one professional association that publishes an educational journal. Many professional organizations are subject specific, such as the International Reading Association, the National Council of Teachers of Mathematics, and the National Science Teachers Association. A similar state organization is usually affiliated with the national group. Other organizations are geared toward children with special needs. See Resource 9.1 for a list of names and websites of recommended professional associations. These organizations publish regular newsletters and journals for their members, with interpretive articles on educational research and practical teaching tips.

Local, state, and national organizations also have annual meetings with speakers, workshops, exhibits, and events. Educational publishers are invited to set up displays. You will leave these conferences with bags of sample materials, freebies, teaching packets that workshop leaders distribute at their sessions, and pages of notes and new ideas. Teaching other teachers about your special skills is an important component of the professional growth process.

Conference attendance gives you an opportunity for professional networking beyond your school and district. Meeting and sharing with both other new teachers as well as veteran teachers from other places provides networking opportunities as well as confirming that you are not alone in your concerns. But most important, you will gain ideas about new programs and techniques that work for others and may work back home for you. Again, check with your administrator to find out ahead of time what conferences your school or district will encourage you to attend and will pay for.

> ## HOW TO BE A PROFESSIONAL TEACHER
>
> - Continue to improve your professional skills by being a lifelong learner:
>   - Read journals.
>   - Attend conferences and conventions. Participate in workshops and in-services.
>   - Keep informed about local, state, and national educational issues.
> - Reflect often on your practice.
> - Keep updated with technology in your instructional practice.
> - Exhibit actions that reflect your belief that all children can learn.
> - Keep student information confidential. Keep student files, reports, and parent communication secure and confidential.
> - Model respectful behavior toward students, staff, and parents.
> - Dress as a professional. Remember that you are both a role model to your students and your school community. You represent the professionalism of your school. Because you expect to be treated as a professional by staff and parents, dress and act professionally at all times.

YOUR TEACHING PORTFOLIO

Many beginning teachers develop professional portfolios. Portfolios are useful for assessing your professional growth and documenting the knowledge, skills, and abilities you have acquired. Portfolios serve as tools for reflection and are a way to thoughtfully document both your teaching practices and your progress toward your goals. You need not feel overwhelmed by the process of creating a portfolio, as it is frequently a component of new-teacher induction programs. As such, you will have the support and guidance of your support provider throughout the process.

As actual artifacts of teaching, portfolios can be conversation starters for you and your mentor, support provider, other colleagues, and your principal. Portfolios can provide a focus for your discussions. Portfolios also work well as a tool for self-reflection—helping you think systematically about your practice, reflect on the issues you face, and learn from experience. They provide direct evidence of what you have accomplished, especially during your first few years.

Allow your portfolio to showcase your best efforts. A showcase portfolio is typically used in employment interviews and in assessment of teaching competency. A portfolio can strengthen your résumé and supplement the interview or tenure process. It provides multiple sources of evidence that you have collected through time, sorted, and refined to reflect your best work. The final, polished presentation portfolio, similar to the artist's portfolio, is an important marketing tool for promoting your skills and abilities.

The portfolio shows your ability to plan and design instruction, create and use instructional materials, and evaluate student learning and your knowledge of content. Developing a portfolio requires you to integrate knowledge, skills, and attitudes acquired from a variety of practical experiences with teaching. It requires you to establish your own standards of excellence and decide how to demonstrate these standards through tangible documents. A portfolio serves as a guide to help you define your values and beliefs about teaching and learning. It helps you reflect on your teaching practices and on what you have observed in your classroom and school. In many states and locales, you will be encouraged to extend the development of your portfolio throughout your induction years of teaching.

In most cases, your school district or induction program will have established criteria detailing the knowledge and skills to be demonstrated in the portfolio with rating rubrics and other assessment forms. You might choose to organize much of the required information into the following eight categories:

1. Organization and classroom management
2. Planning and designing instruction
3. Delivering instruction
4. Incorporating technology into instructional methods
5. Student use of technology
6. Assessment of student learning
7. Communication with families
8. Participation as a member of a learning community

Typically, a portfolio consists of at least one entire teaching unit, including the unit's goals, rationale, sequence of lessons, and learning activities. Using the eight areas of teaching competence listed above as a framework, you can expand your portfolio to exhibit your effectiveness in each area. Specify in detail the learning activities in which you engaged students, and provide samples of your instructional materials and assignments given to your students during the unit. Be sure to include examples of student work with your evaluative feedback. Be careful to remove student names from materials to protect the anonymity of students and their families. You may choose to include photographs of students participating in lesson activities, bulletin boards related to the lesson, models constructed, learning centers, and so forth. Make sure your lesson plans show active learning, a variety of strategies and modalities, and sensitivity to language, cultural, and individual differences.

Don't forget to add links to websites, such as a school and class webpage, and document the ways in which you have incorporated technology into your instruction. Be sure to also include technology projects, parent communication, and a copy of your most current curricula vitae (CV). Your portfolio could also include a videotaped lesson.

It is also important to provide concrete examples of your teaching effectiveness in classroom management and discipline and behavior management strategies. Sample portfolio entries might include descriptions, explanations, samples, and photographs of the following:

- "Our Classroom Rules"
- Parent information letter about rules and consequences
- Effective planning for transition time
- Procedures, routines, and classroom organization
- Class meetings

What should the presentation portfolio look like? There is really no prescribed blueprint for a portfolio. It should reflect your own particular style, focus, and preferences. Four rules of thumb, however, will help you produce a quality document:

1. Use a three-ring presentation binder that allows you to insert materials and move them around.

2. The appearance of your portfolio should be *impeccable* because it is a tangible representation of your personal standards of excellence. It should have laser printing, quality bond paper, and plastic page covers.

3. Begin your portfolio with a title page and table of contents.

4. Be selective in adding the materials. More is not necessarily better.

What Materials Should I Include in My Portfolio?

Your portfolio will begin small and will become more extensive and refined as you get more involved in the professional life of your school and district. Some of the materials will not be developed until you complete your first year of teaching.

- ☐ Title page
- ☐ Table of contents
- ☐ Statement of your philosophy/educational credo
- ☐ Curricula vitae (CV)
- ☐ Professional goals
- ☐ Letters of reference
- ☐ Honors and distinctions (e.g., certificates; award letters; list of achievements such as conference presentations, honorary societies, and other recognitions)
- ☐ Photos of you with your students engaged in whole-group and small-group instruction and related professional activities (each photo should be captioned)
- ☐ Newspaper clippings that cite your achievements
- ☐ The following artifacts can be added as you complete your first year of teaching:
    - o Samples of classroom management plans, techniques, and routines
    - o Sample of unit plans
    - o Sample of lesson plans
    - o Sample of project-based and learning centers plans
    - o Sample of technology projects
    - o Samples of student work with your written feedback and evaluation or grade
    - o Sample tests, rubrics, or assessment and evaluation methods
    - o Videotape of your teaching

Even if your district does not require portfolios, consider keeping one to capture what you do in the classroom and your knowledge and decision making as a professional. Sit down occasionally to review it, reflect on your growth, and move forward in your professional growth and development.

STRATEGIES FOR SUCCESS IN YOUR FIRST YEAR AND BEYOND

The effectiveness of your teaching directly affects students' effectiveness as learners. You must constantly ask yourself if you are creating learning experiences that result in positive outcomes for children. As a beginning teacher, it is easy to get trapped in time and logistic pressures as you manage a myriad of details. One of the realities of school life is that resources are finite and decisions involve compromises. As you allocate that most precious resource—the teacher's *time*—look to your students. Make decisions based on what happens to them. Will they be truly engaged in the learning tasks? Will your classroom provide rewarding social and personal experiences?

It's hard to imagine a more demanding job than teaching. You could easily spend 14 hours a day preparing to teach and teaching. Please don't. Try to establish a point each day when schoolwork stops, even if it is not done. To survive and flourish at teaching, you must find some relaxation time. Enjoy the other important aspects of your life, too. You will have more of yourself to give to your students if you take care of yourself. Feelings of burnout are a prevalent and serious problem for new teachers. Realize that few things are ever totally completed in education. Pace yourself. Beware of not allowing the pressures of teaching to outweigh the positive aspects.

Veteran teachers have developed ways to cope with the pressures of the job. See their suggestions in the box below.

CLASSROOM AND TIME-MANAGEMENT TIPS FROM VETERAN TEACHERS

- Assign each student a partner. When a student is absent, the partner can gather assignments that the absent student has missed. Have partners exchange phone numbers.
- When you ask students to check each other's papers, have checkers sign their names at the bottom. Students are more careful when their names are on the checked assignments.
- Train students to place assignments, right side up, with their names at the top, into a Completed Work basket or bin. Have a labeled basket for each subject, so papers are sorted for you.
- When you put students' names into your grade book (in hard copy or online), number the names in consecutive order. Have students always write their name *and number* on their papers. You (or a student) can quickly put papers in order. You can easily see which papers are missing; and when they are corrected, they will be in numerical order to readily mark into your grade book.
- Ask for clerical (non-confidential) help from parents. Choose tasks for parents to do at home on a weekly or monthly basis, such as typing newsletters, preparing teaching materials, and preparing book club orders.
- Teach students to do as many clerical tasks (attendance, lunch count, etc.) as possible.

(Continued)

(Continued)

- Designate one spot on the whiteboard on which you write what students should do as soon as they enter the classroom. Teach students to look there and begin without wasting time. It will give an orderly beginning to your class at the start of the day and after recess and lunch breaks. Have a system, so students know what to do each day.
- Write frequently used directions on a chart instead of the chalkboard. When needed, hang up the chart. This is a good idea for assignment guidelines, book report outlines, paper headings, studying tips (e.g., survey, question, read, recite, review—SQ3R), and many other procedures or reminders.
- Designate one day a week, usually Friday, to send student work home to parents.
- Have available important information that you (or your substitute) needs regularly.
- Review your To Do list every morning. Check off tasks as they are completed.
- Save time by designing your own lesson plan book. Take a page from the standard book and write in times, subjects, morning routine, recess, lunch, special classes, and other constant features. Duplicate this page, so when you make your weekly lesson plans, you need only add the specific lesson topics for that week.
- Place extra copies of student worksheets in a Homework Box. Students who lost or forgot their copies can easily take another. Also, students can help themselves for extra practice or extra credit.
- Identify your supplies (pencils, scissors, markers, etc.) with a masking or colored tape strip.
- Use an overhead projector transparency to write class notes or graphic organizers during presentations. This way, you can date and save them, use them again, and/or review them on another day.
- Refile your materials as soon as possible, so you can find them later.
- Post a daily schedule.
- Make two blank copies of each student worksheet for your own use—one to file for future reference and one to make an answer key.
- Laminate frequently used materials for reuse in subsequent years.
- Keep a personal care kit at school (include aspirin and a needle and thread).
- Stamp your name inside all the books you use, both class sets and personal books you lend to students. If a book is misplaced, it finds its way to your faculty mailbox.
- Maintain an index card file or an online file for each of your students to make notations on behavior (both positive and troublesome) and to record parent contacts. This information will become a great resource in determining grades and when talking to parents.
- Create a class webpage. Post the daily schedule, homework assignments, important dates, events, and conferences on it. Include pictures and videos of events, samples of student work, and an iCal for parents to sign up to help in the classroom.

I touch the future . . .

I teach.

—Christa McAuliffe

RESOURCE 9.1

Professional Associations of Interest to Educators

American Educational Research Association (AERA)
202–238–3200
http://www.aera.net

Association for Supervision and Curriculum Development (ASCD)
800–933–ASCD
http://www.ascd.org

Council for Exceptional Children (CEC)
888–232–7733
http://www.cec.sped.org

International Reading Association (IRA)
800–336–7323
http://www.reading.org/

National Association for the Education of Young Children (NAEYC)
800–424–2460
http://www.naeyc.org

National Center for Early Development and Learning (NCEDL)
919–966–7180
http://www.fpg.unc.edu/ncedl/

National Center for Education Statistics (NCES)
202–502–7300
http://www.nces.ed.gov/

National Council for Social Studies (NCSS)
301–588–1800
http://www.socialstudies.org/

National Council of Teachers of English (NCTE)
217–328–3870
http://www.ncte.org/

National Council of Teachers of Mathematics (NCTM)
800–235–7566
http://www.nctm.org/

National Education Association (NEA)
202–833–4000
http://www.nea.org

Learning Forward
972–421–0900
http://www.learningforward.org

National Science Teachers Association (NSTA)
703–243–7100
http://www.nsta.org

Teachers of English to Speakers of Other Languages (TESOL)
888–547–3369
http://www.tesol.org

United States Department of Education
800–USA–LEARN
http://www.ed.gov

References and Suggested Reading

Anderson, L. W., & Krathwohl, D. R. (Eds.). (2001). *A taxonomy for learning, teaching, and assessing: A revision of bloom's taxonomy of educational objectives.* New York: Addison Wesley Longman.

Calkins, L. M. (1994). *The art of teaching writing.* Portsmouth, NH: Heinemann.

Canter, L., & Canter, M. (1992). *Assertive discipline: Positive behavior management for today's classroom.* Santa Monica, CA: Lee Canter & Associates.

Canter, L., & Canter, M. (1993). *Succeeding with difficult students.* Santa Monica, CA: Lee Canter & Associates.

Codell, E. (1999). *Educating Esme: The diary of a teacher's first year.* Chapel Hill, NC: Algonian Books.

Cohen, E. G. (1994). *Designing groupwork: Strategies for the heterogeneous classroom* (2nd ed.). New York: Teachers College Press.

Costa, A. L. (Ed.). (1991). *Developing minds: A resource book for teaching thinking* (Rev. ed.). Alexandria, VA: Association for Supervision and Curriculum Development.

Cross, K. P., & Steadman, M. H. (1996). *Classroom research: Implementing the scholarship of teaching.* San Francisco: Jossey-Bass.

Delpit, L. (1995). *Other people's children: Cultural conflict in the classroom.* New York: The New Press.

Developmental Studies Center, Child Development Project. (1995a). *That's my buddy! Friendship and learning across the grades.* Oakland, CA: Author.

Developmental Studies Center, Child Development Project. (1995b). *Ways we want our class to be: Class meetings that build commitment to kindness and learning.* Oakland, CA: Author.

DiGiulio, R. (1995). *Positive classroom management: A step-by-step guide to successfully running the show without destroying student dignity.* Thousand Oaks, CA: Corwin.

Farkas, S., Johnson, J., & Foleno, T. (2000). *A sense of calling: Who teaches and why.* New York: Public Agenda.

Federal Interagency Forum on Child and Family Statistics. (2009). *America's children: Key national indicators of well being 2009.* Retrieved June 7, 2010, from http://www.childstats.gov/americaschildren/index.asp.

Fisher, C. W., Filby, N. N., Marliave, R., Cahen, L. S., Dishaw, M. M., Moore, J. E., et al. (1978). Teaching behaviors, academic learning time, and student achievement: Final report of phase III-B: Beginning teacher evaluation study. In *Beginning teacher evaluation study technical report* (Tech. Rep. No. V-1). San Francisco: Far West Regional Educational Laboratory.

Good, T. L., & Brophy, J. E. (2000). *Looking in classrooms* (8th ed.). Boston: Allyn & Bacon.

Hirsch, S. (2009). A new definition: NCSD opens the door to professional learning. *JSD Learning Schools, 30*(4), 1–16.

Hunter, M. (1994). *Enhancing teaching.* Englewood Cliffs, NJ: Macmillan.

International Society for Technology in Education. (2010a). *National educational technology standards and performance indicators for teachers 2008.* Retrieved June 7, 2010, from http://www.iste.org/Content/NavigationMenu/NETS/ForTeachers/2008Standards/NETS_T_Standards_Final.pdf.

International Society for Technology in Education. (2010b). *National educational technology standards for students 2007.* Retrieved June 7, 2010, from http://www.iste.org/AM/Template.cfm?Section=NETS.

Jencks, C. (1972). *Inequality: A reassessment of the effects of family and schools in America.* New York: Basic Books.

Johnson, D., Johnson, R., & Holubec, E. (1994). *Cooperative learning in the classroom.* Alexandria, VA: Association for Supervision and Curriculum Development.

Kellough, R., & Roberts, P. (1994). *A resource guide for elementary school teaching: Planning for competence.* Englewood Cliffs, NJ: Macmillan.

Kendall, J., & Marzano, R. (1996). *Content knowledge: A compendium of standards and benchmarks for K–12 education.* Alexandria, VA: Association for Supervision and Curriculum Development.

Koenig, L. (1995). *Smart discipline in the classroom: Respect and cooperation restored* (Rev. ed.). Thousand Oaks, CA: Corwin.

Kronowitz, E. (1996). *Your first year of teaching and beyond* (2nd ed.). White Plains, NY: Longman.

Miller, W. H. (1996). *Alternative assessment techniques for reading and writing.* West Nyack, NY: Center for Applied Research in Education.

Mitchell, R. (1992). *Testing for learning: How new approaches to evaluation can improve American schools.* New York: Free Press/Macmillan.

Moran, C., Stobbe, J., Baron, W., Miller, J., & Moir, E. (1992). *Keys to the classroom.* Thousand Oaks, CA: Corwin.

National Center for Education Statistics. (2009). *Digest of educational statistics.* Retrieved June 7, 2010, from http://nces.ed.gov.

National Staff Development Council. (2001). *Standards for staff development.* Retrieved June 7, 2010, from http://www.nsdc.org/standards/index.cfm.

Niesyn, M. (2009). *Best practices in literacy instruction kindergarten through grade five: An eight-week professional development in service.* Saarbrücken, Germany: VDM.

No Child Left Behind Act of 2001, 20 U.S.C. § 6319 (2008).

North Central Regional Education Laboratory. (2004). *Teacher education and technology planning guide.* Retrieved June 7, 2010, from http://www.learningpt.org/pdfs/tech/guide.pdf.

Northwest Regional Educational Laboratory. (1982). *How to increase learning time: A tool for teachers.* Portland, OR: Northwest Regional Educational Laboratory Technical Assistance Center.

Northwest Regional Educational Laboratory. (1986). Module III: Instructional management. In *Training model for academic efficiency* (pp. 122–216). Portland, OR: Author.

Palmer, P. J. (1998). *The courage to teach.* San Francisco: Jossey-Bass.

Pearson, M. J., & Honig, B. (1992). *Success for beginning teachers: The California new teacher project.* Sacramento: California Department of Education, Commission on Teacher Credentialing.

Podesta, C. (1990). *Self-esteem and the six-second secret.* Thousand Oaks, CA: Corwin.

Porro, B. (1996). *Talk it out: Conflict resolution in the elementary classroom.* Alexandria, VA: Association for Supervision and Curriculum Development.

Raffini, J. P. (1996). *150 ways to increase intrinsic motivation in the classroom.* Needham Heights, MA: Allyn & Bacon.

Schell, L., & Burden, P. (1992). *Countdown to the first day.* Washington, DC: National Education Association.

Shannon, S. M. (2007). *Please don't label my child.* New York: Rodale.

Shonkoff, J. P., & Phillips, D. A. (Eds.). (2000). *From neurons to neighborhoods: The science of early childhood development.* Washington, DC: National Academy Press.

Snow, C. E., Burns, M. S., & Griffin, P. (Eds.). (1998). *Preventing reading difficulties in young children.* Washington, DC: National Academy Press.

Stansbury, K., & Zimmerman, J. (2000). *Lifelines to the classroom: Designing support for beginning teachers.* WestEd & Office of Educational Research and Improvement. Retrieved June 7, 2009, from http://www.wested.org/online_pubs/tchrbrief.pdf.

Temple, C., Martinez, M., & Yokota, J. (2006). *Children's books in children's hands: An introduction to their literature* (3rd ed.). Boston: Pearson.

Tomlinson, C. A. (2001). *How to differentiate in mixed-ability classrooms* (2nd ed.). Alexandria, VA: Association for Supervision and Curriculum Development

Topping, K. (2001). *Peer assisted learning: A practical guide for teachers.* Newton, MA: Brookline Books.

Unger, H. G. (1996). Coleman report. In H. G. Unger (Ed.), *Encyclopedia of American education* (Vol. 1, p. 213). Washington, DC: Brookings Institution.

U.S. Census Bureau. (2000). *Census 2000 special reports.* Retrieved June 7, 2010, from http://www.census.gov/population/www/cen2000/briefs/index.html#sr.

U.S. Department of Education. (2001). *The No Child Left Behind Act of 2001.* Retrieved June 7, 2009, from http://www.ed.gov/policy/elsec/leg/esea02/index.html.

Warner, J., & Bryan, C. (1995). *The unauthorized teacher's survival guide.* Indianapolis, IN: Park Avenue.

Williamson, B. (1988). *A first-year teacher's guidebook for success: A step-by-step educational recipe book from September to June.* Sacramento, CA: Dynamic Teaching.

Wlodkowski, R., & Jaynes, J. (1990). *Eager to learn: Helping children become motivated and love learning.* San Francisco: Jossey-Bass.

Wolfe, P. (1988). *Catch them being good: Reinforcement in the classroom* [Video series and manual]. Alexandria, VA: Association for Supervision and Curriculum Development.

Wong, H., & Wong, R. (1991). *The first days of school: How to be an effective teacher.* Sunnyvale, CA: Harry R. Wong.

Wright, S. P., Horn, S. P., & Sanders, W. L. (1997). Teacher and classroom context effects on student achievement: Implications for teacher evaluation. *Journal of Personnel Evaluation in Education, 11,* 57–67.

Notes

Notes

Notes

Notes

Notes

CORWIN

A SAGE Company

The Corwin logo—a raven striding across an open book—represents the union of courage and learning. Corwin is committed to improving education for all learners by publishing books and other professional development resources for those serving the field of PreK–12 education. By providing practical, hands-on materials, Corwin continues to carry out the promise of its motto: **"Helping Educators Do Their Work Better."**